Liberty H. Bailey

Liberty Hyde Bailey letters to Walter Deane, 1883-1929

Liberty H. Bailey

Liberty Hyde Bailey letters to Walter Deane, 1883-1929

ISBN/EAN: 9783337393632

Printed in Europe, USA, Canada, Australia, Japan

Cover: Foto ©ninafisch / pixelio.de

More available books at **www.hansebooks.com**

July 9.

My Dear Deane:

You are correct. The Carex is typical C. pallescens. It is one of our best marked, and most constant species so far as characters are concerned. The st. spikes are short stalked. You are doing well; go on.

Your Galium is as near trifidum as you can get it I guess, although its size & slender habit look towards var. pusillum. It also has an approach to the deflexed leaves. The real trifidum is in herb. from N.Y. and other places.

Will be very much pleased to aid you in your work on Carex. Will also be glad of the spec. you have in press for me. Yours ever,

[illegible]

NOTHING BUT THE ADDRESS CAN BE PLACED ON THIS SIDE

1883

Mr. W. Deane,
Shelburne

Botanic Garden of Harvard University,

Cambridge, Mass., July 7, 1883

My Dear Deane:

Much obliged. Do it again. Your carex is already mounted and labelled C. Monile Tuck. Had never seen it before. The perigynium is conspicuously few-nerved, and the sterile spikes are stalked, or at least the terminal one is. The stalk is usually thought to begin at the next spike below in such a case. Put a few spec. in press for me, and look out for carices and grasses, etc.

Was glad to know that you are securely settled. I almost envy you your vacation in the fields and woods. But don't keep your good times all to yourself. Let me know about it often, not forgetting, of course, to give a full account of our mutual friends, the plant. Mrs. B. declares that I will turn into a Carex. I tell her it will be all carex if I do.

No chance for cold feet here now. Thermometer is reaching for the hundredth degree, and I feel as though it had got there.

Remember me to Mrs. D.

Yours hotly,

L. H. Bailey, Jr.

Cambridge, July 11. [illegible]

My Dear Deane: I [illegible] still[illegible]

The Carex you sent me as lupulina (the first one) is C. tentaculata, Muhl. As near as I can judge from the imperfect spec. the crinita is alright. If the sheaths are rough it is gynandra. No. 3 is one of the forms of perplexing stellulata. The assertion that that sp. occurs at "L. Superior & N." is a mistake. It is common here. That section of Carex is the most perplexing of all. You will doubtless have occasion to puzzle over the numberless forms of straminea, and of scoparia.

No. 4 is intumescens; No. 5 lupulina.

The Eriophorum seems to be good paucinervium. The other sp. is alpinum.

Lemnas in flower.

Don't overburden yourself with plants for me.

Summer school goes off calmly. Some 5 or 6 pupils. Mrs. B. is indulging in it.

Let me hear from you often. Regards to Mrs. D. You will see my wife's sentiments at the head of this letter.

Yours indelibly,

L.H.B. Jr.

Now let me ask you a question. I want to do some teaching next College year. Do you know of any institution near Boston or Cambridge where a poor, ignorant devil would stand a chance of an opportunity to teach botany or botany and some other natural science? Can get enough time from my work here to attend to such things after August.

You will be pleased to learn that I'm not yet starved to death. In fact I am increasing in muscle & ill-temper.

Nothing of importance in the garden only Monarda didyma, Hypostegia and millions of

me
7. Juncus Effusus

The Microstylis is certainly rare. Have never seen it. The herb. needs good spec. of it. Your card in relation to Asclepias is rec'd but the spec. is not yet. May it not be A. incarnata?

Dr. Gray is quite ill with dysentery. Has not been up to-day. The physician thinks he can get up to-morrow.

Have not looked up the Dalibarda yet.

More anon,

L. H. B. Jr.

Mr. W. Deane, 1883

Shelburne,

N. Hampshire

9. C. Vulgaris. Fries

10. C. Stricta var. strictior.
The var. is new to me. One
spec. in herb. like it from
Oakes from base of White Mts.
The lower spikes were fertile I think.

11. Eleocharis palustris, R. Br.

12. Scirpus sylvaticus or atrovirens.

I've mislaid No. 8. Will run
across it in some of my pockets
likely. Did not look at it closely
but think it is C. scoparia.

Dr. Gray is just getting
around. Have not shown
him the Asclepias yet. I
think it is good A. incarnata.
Don't worry about troubling
me. Working on Goad
again. In haste,

July 17. '83. L. H. B. Jr.

NOTHING BUT THE ADDRESS CAN BE PLACED ON THIS SIDE.

1883

Mr. Walter Deane,

Shelburne,

New Hampshire

Eriophorum Virginicum.
(1) Setaria viridis
I name spec. of Viola renifolia for you
I often find Asc. incarnata without the hairy lines. The norms on
match spec. in herb. Equisetum
arvense is frequently 3-sided. There
are such spec. in herb. You did
not send me your Briza media.
Dr Gray seems to be almost fully recovered. Don't spend too much
time on Betulas &c. You ought to
find some alpine Carices &
grasses. Put in some of all you
find anyway. Tough for a mar-
ried man to botanize with the girls.
I'd give my old shoes to go into the mts.
with you. Send me all the
Carices you wish. Vermont spec.
of Dalibarda from Pringle show
fine Cleistogamous flowers.
Am at work nearly all the
time on food. Have some
things in press for you. Mrs. B.
goes to Mich. next week, so I'll be
a bach. again. Yrs &c L.H.B. Jr.

POSTAL CARD.

NOTHING BUT THE ADDRESS CAN BE PLACED ON THIS SIDE.

CAMBRIDGE
JUL 27
10 A.M.
MASS.

ONE CENT

Mr. Walter Deane, 1883

Shelburne. N. Hampshire.

July 20, '83

Carex No. 8. is good scoparia.
Your Asclepias is incarnata.
Will you get me all
the spec. you can of the
various forms of Betulas
& Alnuses — one or two
spec. of each peculiar form
with some notes on their
sizes and general appearances?
Would like some of the high
alpine forms of B. pumila &
glandulosa. If any of the wood
or branches appear peculiar
send me a section & I'll
bear expense. Your Oz-
morhiza is brevistylis. Will
look up the Equisetum. Dr.
G. is improving slowly.

L. H. B. Jr.

POSTAL CARD.

NOTHING BUT THE ADDRESS CAN BE PLACED ON THIS SIDE

CAMBRIDGE MASS. JUL 20 5 PM

U.S. POSTAGE ONE CENT

Mr. Walter Deane,

Shelburne,

N. Hampshire

Botan. Gardens, Cambridge, Aug. 4, 83

My Dear Deane:

Your Brassica is B. campestris, L. Your questions involve a good deal of study, and part of them cannot be answered satisfactorily. Brassica campestris is a cosmopolitan species, occurring in many widely different and perplexing forms. It occurs in the form you send me as an abundant weed in Europe. B. Napus, or B. campestris var. Napus is of doubtful origin. It is supposed to have come from B. campestris by many or most authors. Your spec. cannot be var. Napus as I understand it, as the distinguishing character of that variety is its napiform root. I do not doubt but that the turnip and ~~cabbage~~ rutabaga were originally annuals, and that cultivation has prolonged the period of growth into two years. They are a sort of pseudo-biennials to make the most of them. Turnips often seed the first year if sown early, and allowed to remain in the ground. Your plant is one form of the multiform Brassica campestris and is probably an introduction from Europe in its present condition and not a deteriorated turnip. That is about all I can say about it. I have not consulted DeCandolle's late work on the subject

(2) Setaria glauca (3) Juncus ——

(4) Dulichium spathaceum

I call your sagittaria the var. angustifolia. The section you enclose is undoubtedly insect work. Amphicarpaea and Amphicarpum have cleistogamous fls. Your bean was peculiar — a double crop, or double pistil rather. Have not yet tried to identify the Melilotus. They are numerous and difficult & I doubt if I can make much of it. Was sorry to hear of your misfortune. Your last letter says you are improving, however, and I trust you are O.K. by this time. Will be glad to see you back.

Do you know this? I enclose spec. of N. flexilis and a new one which I found at Spot Pond last Wednesday. Will you look sharp into every pool for such spec. for me? You will find some slender things smaller than these probably; if so don't fail to save them. Found many nice things at Spot Pond — Elatine Americana among them. The Naiad is new to America. I am intending to try my hand at revising the genus. It is mixed. Collect everything peculiar even if you have no idea what it is. Have a few things dried for you. Regards to Mrs. D.

BOTANIC GARDEN OF HARVARD UNIVERSITY,

CAMBRIDGE, MASS. Sept. 6, 1853

Mr. Deane.

Dear Sir:

I have been unable to find any reference to a European May-Flower. Prior, in his exhaustive "English Plant Names", makes no mention of any plant known by that name, and there is no reference to such a name in Ray's "Historia Plantarum (1704), nor in Gerarde, 1633, nor in Clusius, 1601, nor in the still older works which I have consulted. Dr. Gray informs me that there is no native of Europe known as May-Flower. There is a "May" however, well-known in England. It is the Crataegus Oxyacantha, or English Haw-Thorn. The plant known to us as May-Flower (the Epigaea repens) is somewhat cultivated in England and has been many times described in English works, but I can nowhere find any reference to it as May-Flower. Edwards, in Botanical Register 1817, even says that it is known in America as "Ground Laurel." The plant was introduced into England in 1736 by Peter Collinson who no doubt obtained it of his friend John Bartram.

Yours resp'y, L. H. Bailey, Jr.

My Dear Deane:

I've been sick for some days, some of the time sick abed, and have not answered your letter. I am just trying to work again this morning.

(5). Calamagrostis Canadensis

(4) Glyceria Canadensis

Aster is A. Radula

Dr Gray says "It is possible that the Brassica is a deteriorated turnip, but it is not probable. It is probably an introduction from Europe."

I did not know the sp. of Juncus. Have not examined the Panicum as it came to the house when I was sick. It has the appearance of P. xanthophysum. It is certainly one of its near neighbors if not xanthoph— itself.

The naiads grow usually in shallow

water.

Things are going on slowly here. Mrs. B. did not go West as she expected, but intends to go next Monday. Will be glad to see you back. Summer class closes next Friday or Saturday. I made a pleasant trip to the Mystic Ponds last week.

Yours as ever,

L. H. Bailey, Jr.

BOTANIC GARDEN OF HARVARD UNIVERSITY,

CAMBRIDGE, MASS., Sept. 27 1883

Mr. Chas. Deane.

Dear Sir: I should have answered your queries regarding "Mayflower" sooner had I not been so busy moving and resettling.

It will be impossible for me to give you any light upon the first use of the word *Mayflower* to designate Epigaea *repens*. All the early botanical writings were in Latin and gave no English names. The first work in English giving any description of our plants is Josselyn, and I believe he mentions no mayflower, and moreover says nothing about any plant which could answer to it. Even Manassah Cutler, who compiled a flora of Mass. in 1785, does not mention it. The early Latin descriptions are usually vague and insufficient for determination. Cadwallader Colden, who in 1742, compiled a list of the plants growing in "Provincia Noveboracensi Americes" north of Virginia that I find.

The plant was collected, however, and sent to England as early as 1650 by Rev. John Banister of Virginia. Banister made a catalogue of Virginia plants which was published in Ray's Historia Plantarum in 1704. At that day plants were not named as now — a long ablative description serving to distinguish them. Banister called the plant: "Pyrola repens foliis scabris, flore pentapetaloide fistuloso" In 1720 Plukenet figured the plant, giving Banister's name. In 1739 Gronovius in his Flora Virginica called the plant: "Arbutus foliis ovatis integris, petiolis laxis longitudine foliorum". In 1753 Linnaeus published his Species Plantarum in which he adopted the binomial system of nomenclature. He then named the plant Epigaea repens.

This gives you some of the Latin bibliography of the plant. Of its

Townshend, Windham Co., Vt.
July 28, 1884

My Dear Deane:

We are trying our best to find enough to amuse ourselves with. It is still and lonesome up here, and we will probably get enough of it by the end of this week. The season has been exceedingly dry here, an unfortunate circumstance both to the farmer and the botanist. There is little in the woods but dry leaves. The plant which I had in mind as the most desirable thing I could find here is Carex tentaculata v. gracilis. It is a mountain form. The first day, in a cold wood, I found it and have dried 50 specimens. It is the most beautiful Carex I know. I have also found C. miliacea which I never found before. I have put 20 spec. in press of Botrychium lanceolatum. I find Panicum clandestinum in abundance. I also have one spec. of Ophioglossum vulgatum, 2 of Habenaria lacera, 2 of Trifolium agrarium, and other things too numerous to mention. We want to go to Mt. Stratton before we return. There is said to be a lake on its summit, and I hope to find some Naiads and Potamogetons.

You, of course, are finding much and having a good time. The new Carex (C. teres) will be known as Carex multicaulis, Bailey.

Let me hear from you.

As Ever,
L. H. Bailey, Jr.

My Dear Deane:

Your very welcome letter of the 30th ult. is at hand. Glad to hear that you are doing so well. We go home Wednesday. Thanks for the Scheuchzeria. If you cannot find some specimens of the plant young enough to have tough fruit, I should put some in pockets. It is certainly desirable to have Panicum xanthophysum in abundance. If you have time and room I would like you to press 15 spec. for me. If you have not, do not trouble about it. I have got lots of rubbish. Have not had time to identify nearly all. I never found Spiranthes gracilis until last week. Equisetum scirpoides is a good thing to have in duplicate. If referring to me will help you in any way, I am willing. I am getting a good many mosses. Seymour is to have a set of them and he will determine them for me. I am also getting what parasitic fungi I see for Trelease and Seymour.

I am going to make a list of all the plants I have seen here, with notes. I have looked the flora over pretty well for a hasty glance.

Let me hear from you often. Address to Cambridge.

Truly Yours,

L.H.B. Jr.

My Dear Deane:

What has become of you? I have not heard if you reached Shelburne right side up. I am getting along nicely with my new work. No botanical work done since I returned from Vt. of any account. Let me hear from you.

Aug. 23. L. H. Bailey, Jr.

POSTAL CARD.

NOTHING BUT THE ADDRESS CAN BE PLACED ON THIS SIDE.

Mr. Walter Deane,
Shelburne, N. H.

Aug. 28, '84

Your letter and plants at hand. Prof. Scribner is here and he pronounces your Calamagrostis, C. Langsdorfii. Dr. Gray is not here but your Solidago is what I have always called S. speciosa v. angustata.

Will be glad to see you home. The Calamagrostis will be a good thing to have.

Yrs &c.,

L. H. Bailey, Jr.

NOTHING BUT THE ADDRESS CAN BE PLACED ON THIS SIDE.

Walter Deane,
Shelburne,
N. H.

Care of
A. E. Philbrook.

Lansing, Mich., Jan. [illegible]

My Dear Deane— We arrived here at noon. Snow plenty and weather cold. Mr. Smith and I [illegible] were [illegible] [illegible] [illegible] [illegible] [illegible] [illegible] the [illegible] their bodies not being in condition to bring home. [illegible] of the horses were found [illegible] [illegible] [illegible]. The harnesses were [illegible] eaten off by wolves. A [illegible] account from the brother, [illegible] says [illegible] [illegible] [illegible] [illegible] in first [illegible] [illegible] [illegible] [illegible] [illegible] [illegible] [illegible] he started alone in search of the party. He was [illegible] about for a day [illegible] [illegible] [illegible] [illegible] [illegible] [illegible] [illegible] snow [illegible] [illegible] laid [illegible] [illegible] [illegible] [illegible] [illegible] [illegible] [illegible] here. [illegible] is coming [illegible] [illegible] it.

[illegible] [illegible] [illegible] [illegible] 1190 [illegible] [illegible]. Write.

[illegible]

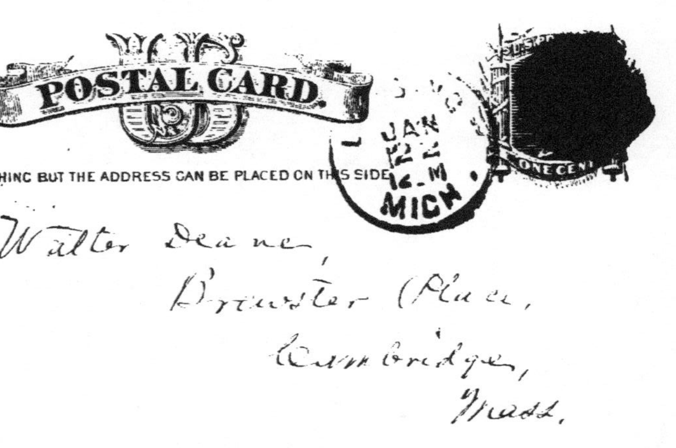

Walter Deane,
Brewster Place,
Cambridge,
Mass.

My Dear Deane:

I had intended to write you before this, but we have been so busy getting settled that I could think of nothing else. We are now living in our neat little cottage at the College. We are not settled but we are here nevertheless. I entered upon my duties as Professor of Horticulture and Landscape Gardening last Monday. Term does not open for three weeks yet, but I have taken possession and have rec'd the full burden of the business connected with the Hort. Department. It is probable that there will be no instruction - no teaching in my Department until the summer term - next June. Our house is a small brick cottage, very neat in appearance. It is the only house on the grounds which has a coal furnace. We command a fine view of some parts of the grounds.

You are fortunate in securing Sargent's work. To whom did you send for it?

The latest news from the West say that the brother is getting along well. He has had the nails all pulled from one foot and the decayed flesh cut off but he will lose no toes. The uncle's feet are worse from poor treatment. Mr. Smith and

The Gardens must be lonely enough when both Dr. Gray and Mr. Watson are absent. Did I tell you that my Mann. list contains 1980 plants which are in my herb.? How many have you?

Our weather has been very severe. It is now warmer but snow is still deep.

I have a little matter for you to look up for me;— no hurry. In the library under P find Prior's Names of British Plants and tell me the essence of what he says about the origin of the name whortleberry from "myrtle-berry", or. Is not the specific name of Vaccinium Myrtillus connected with the history of the English name?

We are both pretty well, although Mrs. B. is pretty well tired out.

Give our regards to Mrs. D., and let us hear from you soon and often.

Yours ever

My Dear Deane:

I feel better: I have just finished a lecture which I am to deliver in the State House to-morrow before the Ingham County Horticultural Socy. Of course everybody wants to see the new Professor of Horticulture and the only polite way to get a sight at him is to invite him to lecture. Of course he is chuck full of lectures and can spit one out at any minute. I can imagine the upturned and disappointed faces to-morrow. I have prepared a genuine "talky-talky" about "Illustrations of Intensive Horticulture." The society is a small one, and I do not think that the size of my audience will embarrass me any.

Your two letters, of the 7 and 9th inst. were rec'd to-day, and I was pleased to get them. I had rec'd one before. Accept thanks for the whortleberry business. It is just what I wanted. Here is another question for you: Look in Steudel's Nomenclator Botan. (Reference books) and see if there is any Viola verna.

Pleasant surroundings! Thermometer 19° below zero last night, 5° below the night before, [illegible]° below the night before ... and the wind steering, etc! It requires all our attention to keeping warm in this new house. It seems as if I can see the North Pole sticking right into the window when I get up in the morning. It is warming up out of doors to-night and I hardly think the Hg will go below zero. Snow about 30 inches on the level.

You are certainly to be congratulated on your numerous acquisitions to your library. You are lucky enough in getting so many nice things, and especially the work on Forestry. You should get Rothrock's little Flora of Alaska from the Smithsonian.

Carex stricta includes C. stricta v. striatior. See Notes No. II, Gazette for September. I recalled the plant I named for you.

What is there new in the way of botanical pamphlets, etc? Twice send for the "Dictionary of Altitudes".

Those new shelves were in the library at the Gardens when I came away.

Here I am chatting away with my dear friend a thousand miles away in historic Cambridge. I can hardly refrain from reaching out my hand to shake with him, but the thought of all those cold and forbidding thousand miles teaches me that I cannot do it. Still very

HORTICULTURAL DEPARTMENT,
AGRICULTURAL COLLEGE.

Lansing, Michigan, ...188....

thoughts are there, and I am sure I can see him sitting in his cozy study and conning occasionally ~~the~~ attractive sheets in the herbarium. Certainly, friendship is an endearing tie, and it is hard to stretch it a thousand miles. I hope those miles will someday shorten that we may meet again. But so long as our guardian Uncle Sam will carry our letters, full of our hopes and plans and sorrows and joys, we will know something of each other. When the flowers bloom again I will think of you in every acquaintance I make with them, our mutual friends.

College opens in two weeks or less, Feb. 25. Then my activity must be more active, for I surely must begin my daily lectures. I have selected a fine young man though some years my senior and a graduate of the institution for my foreman.

I must go to bed. Good night. Regards of us both to Mrs. D. Nettie is well.

Write me often; do not wait for me.

Yours ever,

L. H. Bailey, Jr.

Latest news from the west
say that Jay, the brother, is
improving, though not yet
able to walk.

HORTICULTURAL DEPARTMENT,
AGRICULTURAL COLLEGE, ~~Lansing~~, Michigan, Feb. 24 1885

My Dear Deane:

Things are livening up a little here, and the long monotony of a quiet winter is being broken by the classic yells of students. Term opens to-morrow night. I do not know yet if I will have to teach this term, for this spring's Horticulture is elective and no one may care for it. My department is in such bad shape that students will not be much attracted towards it. If I teach it will be by daily lectures! I will send you a Catalogue when a new one is issued — sometime this term.

It has actually thawed all day! Of the last 40 days, 34 have had temperatures below zero, and 15 and 20 degrees below have been nearly a daily occurrence. Nothing of the like was ever known here before.

I scarcely know what Shelburne Notes you refer to unless it be those on the Birches. I do not know where those notes are among my things but I will look for them. Of course you are welcome to them if I can find them.

Thanks for the notes from Chicago Tribune. I return it.

In regard to your Shelburne Lechea, Rev. E. J. Hill writes: "It seems like a slender form of L. minor var. Stricta. None have been reported from the East, so far as I know." You had better look for it again next summer and send a quantity to Mr. Hill.

I will send you in a week or two a little article which will explain the meaning of "Intensive Horticulture"

You must not look for my book for a month and more. The drawings are not yet completed.

I am glad that you are keeping us posted in regard to the aspect of 860 Main St. You must mention any news which will interest us.

Send along your desiderata and I'll file the list away for reference.

The prairie wolves — cayotes — appeared to have attacked the horses which Mr. Smith and his man tied to the willows, but the horses were uninjured. They probably kicked off the wolves. The harnesses, however, showed the prints of the beasts' teeth.

Good for Viola rostrata! Look for it next year, and bear in mind that I haven't it.

Of course I am busy and

Where can I buy Gerarde's Old Herball?

HORTICULTURAL DEPARTMENT,
AGRICULTURAL COLLEGE.

~~Lansing~~, Michigan, Mar. 4, 1885.

My Dear Deane: Now for a Democratic president. Before this reaches you we will have one. Nothing of account transpiring this way, only that our weather has moderated. Our snow is going. It is not over a foot deep on the level now. Have just rec'd Watson's roses, &c. The Smithsonian proposes to charge me 20¢ for Flora of Alaska although it is marked "free" on their Catalogue. I am busy drawing the pictures ~~from~~ for my book. Do you know where Dr. Gray is now? I am anxious to get out of doors and to see things growing. Write. L. H. B. Jr.

NOTHING BUT THE ADDRESS CAN BE PLACED ON THIS SIDE.

Walter Deane,
Brewster Place,
Cambridge,
Massachusetts

My Dear Deane:- Yours of the 1st is awaiting a reply. Your letters are always very welcome, and I begin to think that I ought to have another by this time. I cannot write as promptly as I would like to do. I have a great pile of letters ahead of me now to answer.

Did I ever send you my Notes III on leaves?

Have not yet succeeded in finding your Notes on Birches.

Mr. Hill will no doubt ~~will~~ be glad to hear from you. Use my name at any time you wish in writing to botanists I know.

Your duplicates must be in good order now.

I know that it is often next to impossible to separate Rubus Canadensis and R. villosus, also R. Canadensis and R. hispidus.

Can you not secure for me mature leaves of Petasites vulgaris from the Gardens in May or June?

Your letters are correctly addressed.

I am paying off some of my botanical debts. I am debtor to several botanists, and I am glad to get rid of my duplicates. I am still in debt to E. J. Hill, John Macoun and C. E. Faxon. Macoun sent me a nice lot of Carices. I sent you a few of

I enclose you another.

I shall expect a specimen of that Viola hastata in the Spring.

We are getting along nicely. Weather begins to get warm. No teaching yet.

Can't write more now, but would like to.

Ever your friend,

L. H. Bailey, Jr.

My Dear Deane:

Your plants are at hand. Some of them I could not determine, they were so imperfectly developed. I enclose you the extent of my knowledge concerning them.

I have never seen Mr. Hill. A friend of mine in Chicago described him once to me as a little man and a most agreeable companion. He is a minister. I have no means of putting you on track of any pictures of botanists except Dr. Beal's. I seldom get a reply to inquiries from John Macoun. Yes, I knew some of those Carices were in bad shape. The perigynia were nearly all off C. Torreyi when I sent it, but the species is so very rare that it is desirable in any condition. Sometime when you are at the Gardens will you please look at the C. Torreyi and tell me where are the specimens there are from?

I am much pleased to hear of Mr. Lincoln's recovery. Remember me to him. I should like to have him call on me if ever he comes this use minutes when work upon such a book can be sandwiched in to good advantage? What kind of a book? Just this: A little work giving the origin of all ordinal and subordinal and generic names of American plants. You are just suited for this work. Such a work would be much like Wittstein only much smaller & better. There is such a work for generic names in England. It seeks to render botanical names popular by clothing them with etymological and historic meanings as well as with botanical associations.

Such a book could discuss in one part the ordinal names (and the sub-ordinal), telling when and by whom made, how much they originally embraced, and what are their modern limits as outlined by Bentham & Hooker and other systematists. This part should contain a prefatory discussion on the make-up of ordinal names in general, e.g. the practices in regard to terminations, etc. Part 2 should contain a similar alphabetic discussion of generic and sub-generic names, giving concisely the derivation, original application and by whom made and when, and as many scraps of history of interest. You have excellent helps to a work of this sort, and you could make it the most attractive book of the kind ever written. How I should enjoy doing such work if I had the linguistic ability and the opportunity! Let me hear that you have undertaken it. We both wish to be remembered to you both. Mrs. B is well.

Yours as ever,

L. H. Bailey, Jr.

My Dear Deane:

Mr. Bebb, supposing me to be still at Cambridge, has asked me to trace for him a picture in Old Trautvetter. I send the letter to you, and ask you to do the tracing and send to him. It will be a good thing for you, perhaps, to have Bebb under obligations to you. You may find the paper he refers to among the pamphlets.

Snow going very fast, and mud taking its place. I am longing for a sight of a green plant — no matter what.

That Eleocharis is properly a var. of obtusa. By the way, will you copy for me that varietal description in Patterson's Flora?

Of course I did not think you a bore. Do so again at any time. I am sorry Seymour is so poorly. He is not strong and he ought to be out of there. This climate is not the place for him.

surprised at any time to hear that all is over with her.

The receptacle of the Tanacetum is surely convex, but scarcely enough so to make a good botanical character.

I am going to establish a Caricetum, a Carex garden in which to grow all the Carices I can get. I want very much to get C. straminea var. silicea which grows at Nahant.

As the snow goes off it leaves 100 acres of lawns and buildings bare for me to attend to. I have a good foreman and two more subordinates, and will soon have another.

Am in a hurry. Regards to Mrs. O.

Yours ever,

L. H. Bailey, Jr.

How do you like my new paper and envelopes?

I spoke to Beal for his photo for you.

HORTICULTURAL DEPARTMENT,
AGRICULTURAL COLLEGE.

~~Lansing,~~ Michigan, Mar. 15 1885

Dear Deane: 27 to-day! Yes, I checked off your Carices. Do not trouble
about old Gerarde any more. Keep me posted
in regard to Dr Gray & Mr. Watson. Snow
not nearly all gone, but it is going. Am
getting on finely. Jay Smith, the one so
badly frozen, is home. Can walk quite
well! Am not doing much work on
herb. Haven't time. Yours &c, L. H. B. Jr.

NOTHING BUT THE ADDRESS CAN BE P[illegible] THIS SIDE.

Walter Deane,
Brewster Place,
Cambridge,
Mass.

DEPARTMENT OF
HORTICULTURE AND LANDSCAPE
GARDENING,

Agricultural College, Mich. April 7, 1885

My Dear Deane:—

I am in your debt at least two letters. Here is one of Mar. 28.

Yes, I took a good specimen of your English Carex vulpina. If you have no specimen of it except the one without a habitat, by all means keep that. It will aid you in identifying another. You can get C. praecox on dry hills at Salem, or Dedham. It is ripe about the time that C. Pennsylvanica is. C. E. Faxon, of whom you got the Subulosis, can probably supply you.

Sorry you cannot go at that book. You are just the man for it.

I shall, of course, look for many nice things from Willoughby, if you go there. It would be a nice trip for you.

I have checked from your desiderata Nos. 2788 + 3502. I have put a-

3200, also the sterile form of No. 3204. I am looking for your photo.

Mrs. Hardy is improving of late, and I am beginning to have a little hope. The open weather is undoubtedly helping her. Nettie is pretty busy with housework and the worry over her sister. Her two younger sisters are with us. Her mother is with Mrs. Hardy.

Here is your card with all the information about Carex Torreyi. Many thanks. I like that species. It is very distinct and very rare.

So this is your vacation. I will venture to pounce upon you now that you are out of school. I am anxious to have a number of questions answered altho I am in no hurry. I enclose them and I think you can understand what I want. I hope it will not tax you too

DEPARTMENT OF
HORTICULTURE AND LANDSCAPE
GARDENING,

Agricultural College, Mich., ... 188..

the whole species is now referred to obtusa; at least the var. detonsa is.

I can tell you just where C. straminea v. silicea grows. Where the Lynn beach on the North side of the neck going to Nahant strikes the first upland, the plant grows in abundance. This upland of Nahant is fenced off you remember, and a gateway leads up the hill and to a hotel on the left. Now, the Carex is just to the S. W. of the gateway. It grows in clumps in the loose sand, and it can be readily recognized even as early as this by the old clumps. If you have occasion to go down that way this spring, send me a root. If you should see a clump of a sedge-like plant in any sea sand, you may be pretty sure that it is this plant.

I don't know where Mrs. Deane's book is. She had better go down and look it up.

I suppose the silence of the publishers is due to the fact that the compositors are laboring long with Cornell names and Cornell writing. Nearly all my pictures have been engraved.

We are now in the peroration of a vigorous thunder storm, the first attempt of the season. It is an opportune celebration of the republican defeat yesterday in the contest for Supreme Judge of the State.

Remember us both to Mrs. D.

Yours as ever,

L. H. Bailey, Jr.

DEPARTMENT OF
HORTICULTURE AND LANDSCAPE
GARDENING,

Agricultural College, Mich., ... 188...

Please look up in Boott:—

Is C. membranacea, Hook, referred to C. compacta, Brown?

Where was each originally described? (Give simply Boott's references)

Does Boott say anything about C. hymenocarpa, Drejer? Anything about C. ampullacea var. borealis, Lange? Where is each originally described?

Give me Boott's localities for C. compacta, Brown; also for C. membranacea, Hook, if he keeps it distinct.

What does he say about the affinities of the species? (i.e. CC. compacta, membranacea.)

DEPARTMENT OF
HORTICULTURE AND LANDSCAPE
GARDENING.

Agricultural College, Mich., April 2, 188 5

My Dear D— Have not had time to look at your plants. Busy. Can scarcely eat. 1000 things on hands. Feel well. Getting on nicely. Will write letter when I get time to take long breath.

L. H. B. Jr.

POSTAL CARD.
NOTHING BUT THE ADDRESS CAN BE PLACED ON THIS SIDE.
APR
MICH.
ONE CENT
Walter Deane,
Brewster Place,
Cambridge,
Mass.

DEPARTMENT OF
HORTICULTURE AND LANDSCAPE
GARDENING.

Agricultural College, Mich. April 21, 1885

My Dear Deane:

I think the Agrostis from England is A. alba, as you have it. A. alba and A. vulgaris are not now regarded as distinct by the best graminologists.

You had better show your dubious Aster to Dr. Gray. I am not prepared to give an opinion. One is certainly A. multiflorus. I return one of each.

I should call your Lycopodium L. inundatum v. Bigelovii. However, I am not expert on these things.

I should call Isoetes No. 1 some form of I. echinospora, probably v. muricata. No. 2. is evidently I. lacustris. I have not had much time to put on them.

Your Carex is C. Gayana, both male & female plants.

Please accept thanks for your work on Carex membranacea. It answers my questions.

You had better look for Carex straminea v. silicea about the middle of June — as early as that. Of course much will depend upon the season. You found it in Nantucket later than that, did you not?

You ought to be in our woods now. Lots of Hepatica acutiloba, Erigenia bulbosa (nearly gone now), Cardamine rhomboidea v. purpurea, Dentaria laciniata, Sanguinaria Canadensis, Erythronium.
We have had a few days of nice weather.

I go home to So. Haven in 2 weeks. Term closes then. A week's vacation. Then I begin lectures on Landscape Gardening. Oh dear!

Mrs. Hardy is still gaining, but very slowly. Have read 32 pp. of proof on my little book. Lots of work. Your card came last night. Began to think you had forgotten me.
Glad to hear that [illegible] is hopeful.

Let me hear from you oftener.

L. H. B. Jr.

DEPARTMENT OF
HORTICULTURE AND LANDSCAPE
GARDENING,

Agricultural College, Mich., April 29 188 5

My Dear Deane: Your most excellent photo is just at hand. Accept Thanks. It brings you right into my study. I shall prize it. Isopyrum and Claytonia are beginning to make a show. Am beginning to press again.

Yours ever, L. H. B., Jr.

Walter Deane,
Brewster Place,
Cambridge,
Mass.

My Dear Deane:

Yours of the 30th is at hand. I am glad that you enjoyed the live flowers. I sent you labels. I am out of printed ones.

Carex foenea var. sabulonum =

Carex straminea var. silicea, (See Carex Catalogue).

I have in press for you flowers of Ulmus racemosa. Will get leaves, fruit and bark from the same tree. Two trees grow naturally within a few rods of my house. Have also in press fls. of Ulmus fulva. It is quite common here. I hope to be able now to pay you back a little for your many favors.

I have bought a horse and buggy, so I can go and come at pleasure.

Am glad to hear that Larrabee finds a place to agree with him. Remember me to him.

Mrs. Hardy is worse again, and we are suffering under greater suspense than ever.

Regards of us both to Mrs. Deane. Tell her to get her canvassing bag ready.

Yours ever and forever,

L. H. Bailey, Jr.

Your photo is excellent. It made
me almost homesick to see
you when I got it.

My Dear Deane:-

Your two letters of the 17th & 18th came during my absence. I have been home on a vacation I had a delightful trip.

I was very glad to get the curious Geasters. I gave half of them to Dr. Beal. He was much pleased with them. You must attack Seymour for the name. They are good things to keep.

Was sorry to hear of Mr. Watson's condition. Hope he may improve rapidly. He wrote me that he found no carices in Gautemala.

Glad to hear of Saarabee's improvement. He must be doing some botanizing.

Lloyd has not sent me his addenda.

Vasey has a new pamphlet on grasses.

Yes, I should like the little Carex you are raising.

Can't write more now. Mrs. Hardy is improving. Regards to Mrs. D.

Yours &c L. H. G. S.

DEPARTMENT OF
HORTICULTURE AND LANDSCAPE
GARDENING,

Agricultural College, Mich. June 10, 1885

My Dear Deane:

Yours of the 7th is in my hands. Thanks for your criticisms of my little book. I am glad you are pleased with it.

Now for the things you point out. The word *five* on p. 81 is a slip. I had already noticed it. Most ash ~~flowers~~ trees are *polygamous* — some flowers perfect, some pistillate. I contend that the ovary of Pomaceae is not *inferior* — there is adhesion, but the insertion of the calyx is below the ovary. Dr. Gray prefers to take this view. Surely the apple is not inferior in the sense that the gooseberry is. See Gray's Lessons on the subject.

What difference does it make about your line on branches ~~of~~ with 1/2 cycle? On other cycles the spiral may run in one direction in one specimen and in the opposite direction in another of the ~~same~~ species. It is so with cones, is it not? When I wrote about the cherry fls. I thought first I ought to give the fact in the matter, then I thought cherry trees are common, I have awakened a desire and my readers will examine for themselves. Perhaps I did wrong.

1. Ipomoea Nil, Roth, of the Man. = I. hederacea Jacq.
2. Watson ignores Polygala Senega v. latifolia, probably because it is nothing more than a mere form.
3. Pyrus arbutifolia v. erythrocarpa of Manual = typical P. arbutifolia. European botanists often give no type species, but refer all forms to varieties. e.g.
4. Ditto. Amelanchier Can. = A. Can. v. Botry.

Am well and happy. Beside all my business and overseeing, I have to lecture every other day on Landscape Gardening, have an article to prepare for Nat'l Hist. Soc'y next Friday eve, a lecture before State Horticult. Soc'y for June 24, a stated lecture before faculty and students shortly after, two papers for the year meeting of the A.A.A.S at Ann Arbor in August, and a multitude of articles for agr. papers. However my head is clear and things boom.

Regards to Mrs. D. Both well.

Always — L. H. B. Jr.

My Dear Deane:
I have a few moments now before going to bed to devote to you, although I am tired and sleepy. You have no idea of how busy I am. From half past four or five in the morning until ten at night I am driven, and during daylight I am out of doors most of the time. I have no end of business to attend to. Fortunately, I have a good book-keeper.

The Cardamine Lloyd and I sent you is C. rotundifolia Mx. C. purpurea C&S is a north-western plant, far beyond our limits.

Your perigynia are interesting forms of Carex laxiflora v. plantaginea. Your Salix is good and clear S. rostrata. Well done. I have S. candida in press for you.

all the time, and though too busy to enjoy them as I should, I feel free and happy. How I prefer these gnarled oaks and the multitudes of tender things they shelter to the brick smoke and dirty grime of the city! And the unkempt masses of bushes which shut out my view from my study windows seem more attractive than any coddled flower garden.

But I must go to bed or else not be up to hear the first trill of the robins or to catch the first incense of the morning. You must write me often. Do not wait for me. I always want to hear from you. Regards to Mrs. Watts.

Yours ever,
L. H. [illegible]

DEPARTMENT OF
HORTICULTURE AND LANDSCAPE
GARDENING,

Agricultural College, Mich., June 2, 1885

My Dear Deane: Sent you yesterday a book. Read it through and tell me which part pleases you best. I have been saving Eriophorum vaginatum for you. Will write a letter as soon as I can.

L. H. B. Jr.

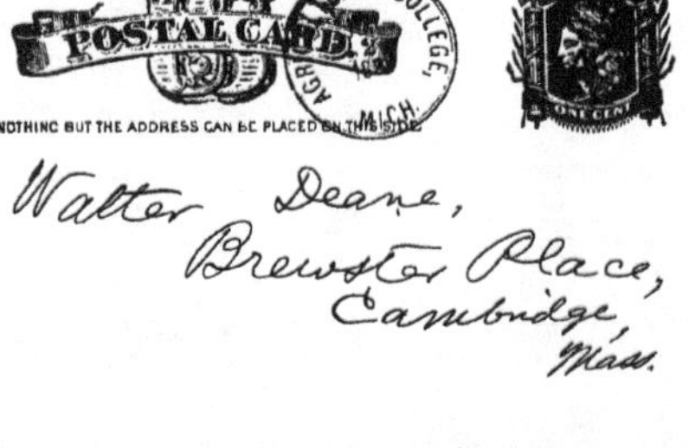
POSTAL CARD

NOTHING BUT THE ADDRESS CAN BE PLACED ON THIS SIDE

Walter Deane,
Brewster Place,
Cambridge,
Mass.

DEPARTMENT OF
HORTICULTURE AND LANDSCAPE
GARDENING,

Have just rec'd some Carices collected by Lieut. Greely in Grinnell Land!!

Agricultural College, Mich., June 24 1885

No. 5 – Correct, but in size, shape & nerving of perig. approaches C. Muhlenbergii.

No. 6. C. straminea v. tenera. This var. must stand.

No. 10. C. laxiflora v. plantaginea never? In type the stam. spike is large, club-shaped & long-stalked, and pist. spikes heavier

No. 11. Poa compressa.

I will keep C. filiformis. It is often called for. Will write letter soon.

Yours &c L. H. B. Jr.

POSTAL CARD.

NOTHING BUT THE ADDRESS CAN BE PLACED ON THIS SIDE.

Walter Deane,
5 - Brewster Place,
Cambridge,
Mass.

DEPARTMENT OF
HORTICULTURE AND LANDSCAPE
GARDENING,

Agricultural College, Mich., June 18 188[illegible]

Carex riparia, C. debilis, C. flava.

Your letter at hand. Will reply in a day or two.

Yours &c
L. H. B. Jr.

POSTAL CARD.

NOTHING BUT THE ADDRESS CAN BE PLACED ON THIS SIDE.

AGRICULTURAL COLLEGE, 188 MTOX

Walter Deane,
Brewster Place,
Cambridge
Mass.

DEPARTMENT OF
HORTICULTURE AND LANDSCAPE
GARDENING.

Agricultural College, Mich. July 1 1885.

My Dear Deane:

In regard to the matter of inferior or superior ovary, I like and hold to the views professed by Dr Gray in his Structural Botany, 5th Ed., page 252. He discusses the apple, and teaches that the outside portion is calyx and that this calyx is inserted below the ovary. The ovary is therefore above the <u>insertion</u> of the calyx and is therefore superior to the calyx. He said that the earlier botanists called such ovaries inferior but he would prefer to discard that term and in such cases substitute the more accurate term, "calyx adherent". You understand that so long as we call the pulp of the apple the calyx so long must we say that in fact the ovary <u>is</u> superior to the calyx — inside of it and above it.

In the sixth Ed. of his Structural Botany Dr Gray makes the bad mistake — it appears to me — of saying that inferiority is not a <u>real</u> circumstance but an <u>apparent</u> one. (See p. 183, paragraph 333, line 5) Hence as the apple ovary is <u>apparently</u> inferior it <u>is</u> inferior! But in the 5th Ed. p. 252, note at bottom, he says that some botanists regard the pulp of the apple as a hollow receptacle, and in the 6th ed. p. 184 par. 336, he is inclined to adopt this view. If this view is correct then the apple ovary is surely inferior to the floral envelopes.

Whoever finds Cardamine ~~rotundifolia~~ purpurea C&S. in Indiana is a little "off." They find the C. ~~rotundifolia~~ rhomboidea var. purpurea which Mr. Watson says is C. rotundifolia. The color of fls. is a poor specific character.

When you get into Carex laxiflora you get into a puzzle. Your Nos. 14 & 15 are C. laxiflora v. latifolia nearly. They approach var. blanda. No. 16 is C. virescens.

I shall surely send you some Carices.

I am glad that you are out of doors again. How long do you remain in Cambridge?

I am glad to hear of Larrabee's improvement.

I stole a couple hours yesterday for a ride to Pine Lake 5 miles away, and for the first time in my life I found Carex filiformis. It was floating on bogs in the lake. Of course I was delighted to find it. I appreciate what you say about your enthusiasm. I can never make a bosom friend of anyone who lacks enthusiasm. The soul of nature and the height of enjoyment do not exist where there is no enthusiasm. And I shall not consent to be called a dreamer because I see in nature much that is enchanting, sublime and poetic. He who looks into nature with admiration lives in a higher world than does he who looks as a critic. (cf. Zelts Africa, i. 137)

Your willow tree may have been attacked last year or year before by plant lice or it may have rec'd some other injury and the hard winter finished it.

Mr. Seymour means nothing. He is absorbed in fungi.

The A.A.A.S. meets at Ann Arbor this year. We shall go.

Lots of business and must close. Do not be afraid of troubling me. Regards to Mrs. D.

Yours always,

L. H. Bailey, Jr.

P.S. I want to use some fish glue — a quart or so. Do you know if I can get it in that quantity and where and for how much?

In card of June 25 you say you send Carices Nos. 12 & 13. I have not rec'd them. C. filiformis v. latifolia = C. lanuginosa.

DEPARTMENT OF HORTICULTURE AND LANDSCAPE GARDENING.

Agricultural College, Mich., July 3, 1885

My Dear Deane:-

No. 17. C. trisperma

18. C. Pseudo-cyperus var. comosa W. Boott (C. comosa Boott) It comes very near being the species.

19. C. bullata Schk. This is a peculiar species. I can always distinguish it at a glance but I cannot define it.

20. C. utriculata,- good find.

I have a job for you: Please look in Boott's Ill. for Carex ustulata. See especially if you can find any mention of the plant ~~being~~ having an androgynous terminal spike. What is the habitat? Also look in Lange's recent Flora of Greenland (Mr. Watson will find it for you) and see if the plant is mentioned. I refer to C. ustulata Wahl. One of the Greeley carices appears to belong to that species.

Does Boott figure C. compacta R. Br.? If not, please look in Pretzel and see if anyone else figures it.

Very hot to-day. Students are going home for the glorious Fourth.

Mrs. Hardy is very feeble.

Regards to Mrs. D. How many books has she sold?

Yours as ever, but dirtier,

L. H. Bailey, Jr.

I am a farmer and ~~gar~~ gardener now-a-days.

GARDENING,

Agricultural College, Mich., July 9

My Dear Deane – I send you to-day a few plants. Some are from the South – specimens which I have recently rec'd. They have not been studied – If you compare them please send me a list of them.

The Carex is rec'd in good order. Thanks.

Yours

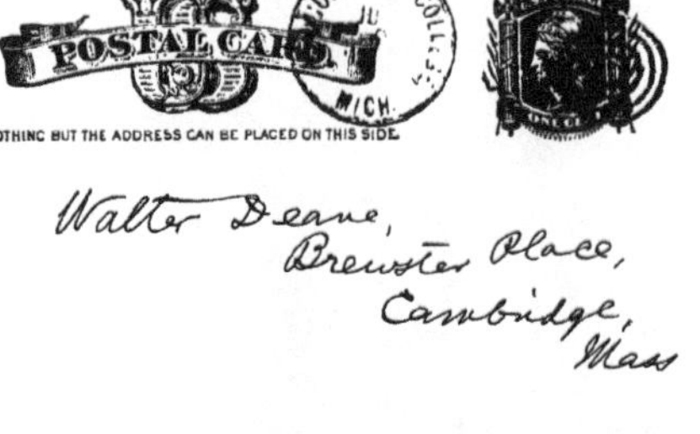
POSTAL CARD
NOTHING BUT THE ADDRESS CAN BE PLACED ON THIS SIDE.
MICH.
Walter Deane,
Brewster Place,
Cambridge,
Mass

DEPARTMENT OF HORTICULTURE AND LANDSCAPE GARDENING.

Agricultural College, Mich., July 18, 1885

My Dear Deane:-

Yours of the 15th is at hand. No. 22 is C. tentaculata. 23 is C. lupulina. The sheaths &c do not furnish any decided marks between these species, but if you will look at ~~the~~ general appearance of the plants you can get at the differences. They look nothing alike. The cylindrical, compactly flowered spikes and nearly squarrose and slender-beaked perigynia of C. tentaculata are very unlike the short, thick, aggregated spikes and the great turgid and thick-beaked ascending perigynia of C. lupulina. 24 is C. ~~tentaculata~~ vulpinoidea.

I am glad Mr. Morong likes my little book. Am pleased that the plants pleased you. Will send you more in the fall.

Did you identify my Euphorbia Esula and Veronica Chamaedrys?

I have rec'd no Greeley carices from Dr Gray, and those I rec'd from Dr Vasey were not numbered. I have written Dr. Gray again in regard to the

Here is your letter of July 6. Did I ever reply to those little carices your lady friend gave you? Both of them – A + B – are young and worthless specimens of C. vulgaris var. hyperborea (C. rigida v. Bigelowii).

I find before me your letter of July 2. Your no. 2. appears to me to be a weak Lolium perenne. I have often seen it just as small. Festuca nutans is abundant here. Ranunculus sceleratus is frequent.

The Carex came alright. It is true var. silicea. Many, many thanks.

The information about Carex ustulata and C. compacta is just what I wanted. Thanks again. C. ustulata is among the Carices Greely collected. Had never seen an American – or rather a Western Hemisphere – specimen before.

You say I have not answered all your nos. I have surely answered them all except the two or three 12 + 13 I think – which you said sent but I never rec'd.

I am about used up with excitement over a long series of investigations which have been had by our faculty to find the guilty parties in a kidnapping scrape and in other scrapes. I hope the thing will soon draw to a close. Yesterday 5 students – 2 seniors, 2 juniors and 1 freshman – were expelled, and four – 1 soph. and 3 freshmen – were suspended. Other expulsions will be made.

Seven years ago I found here the pretty little Erythraea Centaurium. A few days since I visited the locality again and found a few plants. To-day they were nicely in bloom and I put them to press. Of course you shall have one.

I shall be delighted with an Artemisia Stelleriana.

When I say "inferior ovary," I mean that the calyx and petals start above the ovary, as in the case of the gooseberry and huckleberry. I care nothing about the receptacle. Inferiority and superiority is all in reference to the insertion of the floral envelopes in reference to the ovary. In Rosaceae the calyx is inserted below the ovary; therefore the ovary is superior.

I am much gratified at your remarkable promise in sketching. I can readily recognize both you and Mr. Morong in your picture. You certainly had a delightful time. I should enjoy being with you ever so much this summer, but, but! Well, success to you in your new botanizing field. Of course you will enjoy it much and will find many acquaintances in glade and dell.

I once found Blitum virgatum at Cambridge but did not keep my spec. Shall be glad of a spec. Dr Gray or Mr. W. told me that it was once cult. in the Gardens. I have no Gaylussacia dumosa either.

I must close this sketchy letter. Good luck to you and yours!

My Dear Deane:

You are certainly in clover. How I wish I could be with you! We should have a jubilee I am sure. However, I am with you in heart. I shall be rejoiced with a remembrance from among the good things you are harvesting. Look out for Carices and Naiads. Carex arctata, a high northern species, as much like a heavy headed C. canescens, was once found in Northern Vermont. I don't understand about those early numbers you refer to, for, as I wrote you a few days ago, I certainly named the plants as they came and sent you the determinations. Nos. 12 & 13 never reached me.

I shall be especially glad of Primula Mistassinica, (never ~~heard~~ saw good Fragaria vesca from this County), Arabis petraea, Aspidium Braunii, the sterile Carex scirpoidea, Fragaria vesca & Draba arabisans in flower. Shall be glad to see your doubtful Carexes.

My turn to lecture before the Faculty and students occurs next Wednesday. My subject will be: "Man's Imprint Upon Nature." The lecture will be divided into 3 heads: Man the Destroyer, Man the Disseminator, and Man the Improver. Under the first head will be discussed destruction of forests, plants and animals; under second, introduced and adventive plants and animals; under third, improvement of plants and animals.

Mrs. Hardy is in my care. Regards to Mrs. D.

Yours &c.

L. H. B. Jr.

No. 1. [3,000, Mar. 1884.] Agr'l College, Mich.,

~~Boston Public Library, Boylston St., Boston,~~ July 26, 1885

Dear Deane: I have a problem for you:- Please observe alder bushes - and in fact all bushes and trees, especially on cliffs - and see if the leaves on lower limbs are of the same size as on higher, top limbs. I find that I have no Nymphaea odorata. It does not grow here. Can you get me a specimen? Hope you can find. [illegible] up there. Hope you are both enjoying yourselves. Mrs. Harden very low. Yours L. H. Bailey, Jr

POSTAL CARD.

NOTHING BUT THE ADDRESS CAN BE PLACED ON THIS SIDE.

27

Walter Deane,
Willoughby Lake House,
West Burke,
Vermont.

DEPARTMENT OF
HORTICULTURE AND LANDSCAPE
GARDENING.

Agricultural College, Mich. July 20.

Mrs. Hardy died at noon to-day.

L. H. B. Jr.

COMMENCEMENT WEEK.

Sunday, August 16.

BACCALAUREATE SERMON, - - - 3 P. M.

Monday, August 17.

SOCIETY BANQUETS, - - - - - 8 P. M.

Tuesday, August 18.

MILITARY EXERCISES, - - - - - 6 P. M.
CLASS-DAY EXERCISES, - - - - - 8 P. M.

Wednesday, August 19.

COMMENCEMENT EXERCISES, - - - - 10 A. M.
PRESIDENT WILLITS'S INAUGURAL ADDRESS, 3 P. M.
PRESIDENT'S RECEPTION, - - 8 TO 10 P. M.

Thursday, August 20.

ALUMNI.

LITERARY EXERCISES, - - - 10:30 A. M.
BUSINESS MEETING, - - - - - 3 P. M.
BANQUET, ... 8 P. M.

U S POSTAL CARD.

NOTHING BUT THE ADDRESS CAN BE PLACED ON THIS SIDE.

AGRICULTURAL COLLEGE, MICH.

U.S. POSTAGE ONE CENT

Walter Deane,

Shelburne,

N. Hampshire

Care of

A. E. Philbrook.

DEPARTMENT OF
HORTICULTURE AND LANDSCAPE
GARDENING.

Agricultural College, Mich., Aug 5 1885

My Dear Deane:

I am just as glad to hear from you as though I could answer your letters oftener. Your letters from Willoughby have tastes of outdoor life and good botanizing.

As I wrote you in my last note, Mrs. Hardy died July 30. ~~Nettie~~ Mrs. Baily had been with her constantly for some days and I had been there as much as I could. The funeral occurred Saturday. We have been pretty well worn out, but are getting rested up now. But now comes another affliction. The Secretary of the College died yesterday; buried to-morrow.

Mrs. Hardy was conscious to the last. She was fully prepared and was very willing to go.

Here are four of your letters which have not been answered. Thanks for the

the same as the leaves of many violets do. Of course your plantaginea is worth keeping. I want spec: of all the carices you collected up there.

I have plenty of Rhamnus alnifolius but no fruit. Shall be glad of some.

You are very kind to lay aside so many plants for me, but I shall appreciate them, I assure you. Specimens are doubly valuable when they bring dear friendship with them. Fully mature Carex aurea is one of the prettiest carices I know. It is just about equalled, tho' in a different way, by C. [illegible] v. gracilis. Shall be glad of Habenaria obtusata and Aspidium Clintonianum, and especially wild Ribes rubrum.

it over someday.

If larger admission to pleasure you must [illegible] had high enjoyment on the cliffs of Whiteside[illegible]!

Have never seen Sparganium simplex angustifolium.

I have seen Pot. Snap once. Never collected Rhynchospora capillacea. I am especially pleased that you can tell me all about the two Sarraceniae and that you have specimens for me. When you get time write out a statement contrasting one species with another. I have Vaccaria vulgaris in fruit only, from this country.

Juncus A" is probably J. articulatus; "B" is J. nodosus. Your Carex granularis is C. stricta forma [illegible]!!

I go to Ann Arbor Aug. 26 to attend for a week the meeting of the A.A.A.S.

Regards [illegible] to Mrs. D.

Yours as ever

L. H. B. [illegible]

My Dear Deane—

Just time for a line. I have been mounting some carices which I have rec'd and collected this year. I thought I had but a few, but I mounted 144 new sheets and added to 17 old ones! Shall have as many more by Christmas I expect.

I am filling up my herb. with many common things which I did not have. It does one good to see the gaps fill up. I have finally found, pressed and put into my herbarium a specimen of Portulaca oleracea!! Within 20 feet of my door I found a fine specimen of Plantago Patagonica v. aristata. It must have been introduced. I did not have it.

The American Pomological Soc. meets at Grand Rapids Mich., Sep. 7. I am expected to make an exhibit of wild fruits. I want a plateful of Vitis Labrusca and Corylus rostrata. Can you get them for me? I will willingly pay all expense as the Soc'y pays my expenses. The grapes will not be ripe by that time but never mind. Also, can't you send me the dried specimens of the Fragarias by that time?

I shall appreciate the set of plants you are saving for me. Many thanks for the interesting photo of Willoughby. No more now. Mrs. B is getting rested.

L. H. B. Jr.

Thanks for the Naias. It is broad-leaved
N. flexilis.
Commencement occurs next week.

[83 L]

To MICHIGAN STATE AGRICULTURAL COLLEGE, Dr.

18..

DATE	ITEMS.	DOLLARS.	CENTS.

Account against and Receipt issued to

....

....

RECEIPT.

CURRENT EXPENSES.

(Other than Students' Accounts.)

I HEREBY CERTIFY that the within account is correct.

.... 188...

....
Secretary.

Received, Lansing .... *188*...

of ....

.... *dollars and*

.... *cents, in full of the within account.*

DEPARTMENT OF
HORTICULTURE AND LANDSCAPE
GARDENING,

Agricultural College, Mich., Aug. 18 1885

Yes save for me good plates of Vaccinium Can., V. Penn., and V. Vitis-Idaea. Am very busy and about worn out.

L. H. B. Jr.

POSTAL CARD.

NOTHING BUT THE ADDRESS CAN BE PLACED ON THIS SIDE.

AGRICULTURAL COLLEGE
30
1885
H.

Walter Deane,
Care of A. E. Philbrook,
Shelburne
N. Hampshire

My Dear Deane:

I should name Mrs. Dixon's stuff as follows:

\# C. rosea v. minor.
C. echinata Murr. v. conferta Bailey
C. vestita
C. straminea v. chlorostachys Bckl.
C. straminea v. silicea Bailey
C. stricta
C. bullata
[illegible]
[illegible]

The grass from Churchill is Poa serotina.

Your Carex 44 is a ~~short-spiked~~, but common form of C. tentaculata. Will send you good C. tentaculata later.

Should like to try those wild Vacciniums with you. Be sure to send me a good plate of each. I will see ~~that~~ all your expense is paid. Yes, I am greedy for Aspidium fragrans.

I wanted you to send me a list of all

the Florida plants you verify. If you have not the time, never mind it. Miss M. B. Flint lives in Amenia, Dutchess Co., N. Y. She was in Florida last winter. She saw my advertisement in The Gazette and proposed an exchange.

I had hoped to have your plants all looked over by this time but I have been so busy and am so tired with being up nights that I have not done so. To-day I am employed and Monday morning I go to Ann Arbor for a week. So you must forgive me for the delay. I have looked over part of them. Find some mistakes. One Carex you took for Mobile is good and true. C. Tuckermani.

We are well but tired. A letter sent to me at Ann Arbor in care of Botanical Club will probably reach me.

Ever yours,

L. H. Bailey, Jr.

PART TWO.

B.

OFFICERS ELECTED

FOR THE

ANN ARBOR MEETING.

Thursday, August 27, 1885.

PRESIDENT,

H. A. NEWTON of New Haven, Ct.

VICE PRESIDENTS,

A. **Mathematics and Astronomy**—WM. HARKNESS of Washington, D. C.
B. **Physics**—S. P. LANGLEY of Allegheny, Pa.
C. **Chemistry**—W. R. NICHOLS of Boston, Mass.
D. **Mechanical Science**—J. BURKITT WEBB of Hoboken, N. Y.
E. **Geology and Geography**—EDWARD ORTON of Columbus, O.
F. **Biology**—BURT G. WILDER of Ithaca, N. Y.
G. **Histology and Microscopy**—S. H GAGE of Ithaca, N. Y.
H. **Anthropology**—W. H. DALL of Washington, D. C.
I. **Economic Science and Statistics**—EDWARD ATKINSON of Boston, Mass.

PERMANENT SECRETARY,

F. W. PUTNAM of Cambridge, Mass.

GENERAL SECRETARY,

CHARLES SEDGWICK MINOT of Boston, Mass.

ASSISTANT GENERAL SECRETARY,

(Vacancy.)

SECRETARIES OF THE SECTIONS.

A. Mathematics and Astronomy—E. W. Hyde of Cincinnati, O.
B. Physics—B. F. Thomas of Columbia, Mo.
C. Chemistry—F. P. Dunnington of University of Virginia, Va.
D. Mechanical Science—C. J. H. Woodbury of Boston, Mass.
E. Geology and Geography—G. K. Gilbert of Washington, D. C.
F. Biology—J. A. Lintner of Albany, N. Y.
G. Histology and Microscopy—W. H. Walmsley of Philadelphia, Pa.
H. Anthropology—Erminnie A. Smith of Jersey City, N. J.
I. Economic Science and Statistics—J. W. Chickering of Washington, D. C.

TREASURER.

William Lilly of Mauch Chunk.

MEMBERS OF THE STANDING COMMITTEE

FOR THE

ANN ARBOR MEETING.

Past Presidents—James D. Dana of New Haven; James Hall of Albany; Isaac Lea of Philadelphia; F. A. P. Barnard of New York; J. S. Newberry of New York; B. A. Gould of Cambridge; T. Sterry Hunt of Montreal; Asa Gray of Cambridge; Joseph Lovering of Cambridge; J. E. Hilgard of Washington; Simon Newcomb of Washington; O. C. Marsh of New Haven; George F. Barker of Philadelphia; George J. Brush of New Haven; J. W. Dawson of Montreal; C. A. Young of Princeton; J. P. Lesley of Philadelphia.

Vice Presidents of the Last Meeting—H. T. Eddy of Cincinnati; John Trowbridge of Cambridge; J. W. Langley of Ann Arbor; R. H. Thurston of Hoboken; N. H. Winchell of Minneapolis; E. D. Cope of Philadelphia; T. G. Wormley of Philadelphia; E. S. Morse of Salem; John Eaton of Washington.

Officers of the Present Meeting—H. A. Newton of New Haven; Wm. Harkness of Washington; S. P. Langley of Allegheny; W. R. Nichols of Boston; J. Burkitt Webb of Hoboken; Edward Orton of Columbus; Burt G. Wilder of Ithaca; S. H. Gage of Ithaca; W. H. Dall of Washington; Edward Atkinson of Boston; F. W. Putnam of Cambridge; C. S. Minot of Boston; E. W. Hyde of Cincinnati; B. F. Thomas of Columbia; F. P. Dunnington of University of Virginia; C. J. H. Woodbury of Boston; G. K. Gilbert of Washington; W. H. Walmsley of Philadelphia; Erminnie A. Smith of Jersey City; J. W. Chickering of Washington; William Lilly of Mauch Chunk.

From the Association at Large—Chas. H. Rockwell of Tarrytown; E. W. Blake, Jr., of New Haven; R. B. Warder of Lafayette; George I. Alden of Worcester; A. H. Worthen of Springfield; H. N. Martin of Baltimore; Geo. H. Perkins of Burlington; Henry E. Alvord of Mountainville.

LOCAL COMMITTEE OF ARRANGEMENTS.

President, HON. THOMAS M. COOLEY.
Treasurer, CHRISTIAN MACK, Esq.
Secretary, PROF. JOHN W. LANGLEY.
Secretary's Assistant, MR. E. O. GROSVENOR.

GENERAL CITIZENS' COMMITTEE.

1, Mr. E. D. Abel; 2, Prof. C. K. Adams; 3, Mr. A. W. Ames; 4, Pres. J. B. Angell; 5, Mr. H. W. Ashley; 6, Hon. J. M. Ashley; 7, Mr. P. Bach; 8, Mr. J. N. Bailey; 9, Dr. N. Baldwin; 10, Mr. E. Baur; 11, Mr. J. E. Beal; 12, Prof. W. W. Beman; 13, Mr. H. D. Bennett; 14, Dr. W. F. Breakey; 15, Mr. M. H. Brennan; 16, Mr. R. Brown; 17, Mr. H. J. Brown; 18, Mr. J. C. Bullis; 19, Mr. H. Campbell; 20, Prof. B. W. Cheever; 21, Judge N. W. Cheever; 22, Prof. H. N. Chute; 23, Mr. S. M. Clarkson; 24, Mr. J. Clements; 25, Mr. E. W. Coddington; 26, Mr. W. Condon; 27, Prof. M. E. Cooley; 28, Hon. T. M. Cooley; 29, Mr. B. F. Crane; 30, Col. H. S. Dean; 31, Mr. S. Dean; 32, Dr. W. H. Dorrance; 33, Dr. S. H. Douglas; 34, Mr. E. Duffy; 35, Dr. E. S. Dunster; 36, Mr. C. Eberbach; 37, Mr. O. Eberbach; 38, Mr. A. Eisele; 39, Hon. A. Felch; 40, Mr. J. W. Fardon; 41, Prof. H. S. Frieze; 42, Dr. G. E. Frothingham; 43, Mr. E. K. Frueauff; 44, Dr. C. George; 45, Mr. J. J. Goodyear; 46, Prof. C. E. Greene; 47, Mr. L. Gruner; 48, Mr. L. Hall; 49, Mr. G. Haller; 50, Mr. A. W. Hamilton; 51, Judge W. D. Harriman; 52, Prof. M. W. Harrington; 53, Rev. S. Haskell; 54, Mr. H. W. Hayes; 55, Mr. H. B. Henderson; 56, Mr. J. B. Henderson; 57, Mr. W. B. Henderson; 58, Dr. G. A. Hendricks; 59, Prof. A. Hennequin; 60, Dr. W. J. Herdman; 61, Mr. C. E. Hiscock; 62, Mr. D. Hiscock; 63, Mr. E. H. Hudson; 64, Mr. H. Hutzel; 65, Mr. J. T. Jacobs; 66, Prof. O. C. Johnson; 67, Prof. C. N. Jones; 68, Dr. J. Kapp; 69, Mr. A. Kearney; 70, Mr. J. Keck; 71, Mr. T. J. Keech; 72, Hon. E. D. Kinne; 73, Mr. R. Kittredge; 74, Mr. J. W. Knight; 75, Mr. J. C. Knowlton; 76, Prof. J. W. Langley; 77, Mr. J. F. Lawrence; 78, Mr. C. K. McGee; 79, Mr. D. McIntyre; 80, Mr. C. Mack; 81, Dr. D. Maclean; 82, Mr. G. C. Mahon; 83, Mr. E. Mann; 84, Mr. C. H. Millen; 85, Prof. G. S. Morris; 86, Rev. P. Neumann; 87, Mr. G. Oster; 88, Judge P. L. Page; 89, Dr. A. B. Palmer; 90, Prof. W. H. Payne; 91, Supt. W. S. Perry; 92, Prof. W. H. Pettee; 93, Mr. E. A. Phillips; 94, Mr. A. B. Pond; 95, Mr. E. B. Pond; 96, Mr. O. H. Pond; 97, Rev. D. B. Pope; 98, Mr. R. Popkins; 99, Prof. A. B. Prescott; 100, Mr. N. S. Pulcipher; 101, Hon. C. H. Richmond; 102, Mr. D. Rinsey; 103, Mr. J. J. Robison; 104, Prof. H. W. Rogers; 105, Rev. W. H. Ryder; 106, Mr. J. M. Schaeberle; 107, Mr. F. Schmid; 108, Capt. J. F. Schuh; 109, Mr. E. H. Scott; 110, Mr. J. A. Scott; 111, Mr. M. Seabolt; 112, Mr. J. Q. A. Sessions; 113, Prof. H. Sewall; 114, Mr. A. Seyler; 115, Dr. W. B. Smith; 116, Maj. H. Soule; 117, Rev. H. M. Steele; 118, Prof. J. R. Sterrs; 119, Mr. J. L. Stone; 120, Prof. C. H. Stowell; 121, Dr. T. J. Sullivan; 122, Mr. J. E. Sumner; 123, Rev. J. T. Sunderland; 124, Mr. L. D. Taylor; 125, Prof. C. Thomas; 126, Mr. W. A. Tolchard; 127, Mr. E. Treadwell; 128, Dr. V. C. Vaughan; 129, Mr. J. H. Wade; 130, Mr. W. Wagner; 131, Hon. R. Waples; 132, Mr. E. Ware; 133, Mr. B. F. Watts; 134, Mr. W. W. Watts; 135, Prof. C. K. Wead; 136, Mr. W. W. Whedon; 137, Mr. J. M. Wheeler; 138, Prof. A. Winchell; 139, Mr. L. D. Wines; 140, Mr. W. W. Wines; 141, Mr. C. H. Worden.

LADIES' RECEPTION COMMITTEE.

142, Mrs. C. K. Adams; 143, Mrs. J. B. Angell; 144, Mrs. J. M. Ashley; 145, Miss Mary Ashley; 146, Mrs. P. Bach; 147, Mrs. R. A. Beal; 148, Miss Anna Barker; 149, Mrs. W. W. Beman; 150, Mrs. W. F. Breakey; 151, Mrs. H. J. Brown; 152, Miss Matilda Brown; 153, Mrs. N. W. Cheever; 154, Mrs. S. M. Clarkson; 155, Miss Ida Clements; 156, Miss Mary Clements; 157, Mrs. E. W. Coddington; 158, Mrs. N. B. Cole; 159, Miss Anna Condon; 160, Mrs. M. E. Cooley; 161, Mrs. T. M. Cooley; 162, Mrs. B. F. Crane; 163, Mrs. H. S. Dean; 164, Mrs. I. N. Demmon; 165, Mrs. F. B. D. dePont; 166, Mrs. B. L. D'Ooge; 167, Mrs. M. L. D'Ooge; 168, Miss Alice Douglas; 169, Mrs. G. A. Douglas; 170, Miss Kate Douglas; 171, Miss Lulu Douglas; 172, Miss Sarah Douglas; 173, Miss Clara Dunster; 174, Mrs. E. S. Dunster; 175, Mrs. E. Evans; 176, Mrs. J. W. Fardon; 177, Miss Mary Fardon; 178, Miss Carrie Frieze; 179, Mrs. G. L. Ford; 180, Miss Annie Frothingham; 181, Mrs. S. S. Garrigues; 182, Miss Clara Gott; 183, Miss Lulu Gott; 184, Mrs. C. E. Greene; 185, Miss Charlotte L. Hall; 186, Mrs. I. Hall; 187, Mrs. A. W. Hamilton; 188, Miss Mattie Harriman; 189, Mrs. W. D. Harriman; 190, Mrs. M. W.

Harrington; 191, Mrs. W. J. Hardman; 192, Miss Susie Hill; 193, Miss Clementine L. Houghton; 194, Mrs. L. C. Hunt; 195, Miss Sadie Hyde; 196, Mrs. C. A. Jaynes; 197, Miss Elsie Jones; 198, Mrs. E. D. Kinne; 199, Miss Addie Knight; 200, Mrs. G. W. Knight; 201, Mrs. J. C. Knowlton; 202, Miss Millie Knowlton; 203, Mrs. J. W. Langley; 204, Miss Amanda Mack; 205, Mrs. C. Mack; 206, Mrs. D. Maclean; 207, Mrs. C. S. Millen; 208, Mrs. G. S. Morris; 209, Mrs. A. H. Palmer; 210, Mrs. W. S. Perry; 211, Mrs. W. H. Pettee; 212, Mrs. E. B. Pond; 213, Miss Mary L. Pond; 214, Mrs. R. S. Pope; 215, Mrs. A. B. Prescott; 216, Mrs. H. Randall; 217, Mrs. E. A. Rathbone; 218, Miss Louise Rickards; 219, Mrs. C. H. Richmond; 220, Miss Mary A. Richmond; 221, Mrs. H. W. Rogers; 222, Mrs. H. Wade Rogers; 223, Miss Julia Rominger; 224, Miss Matilda Sager; 225, Miss Mary Scott; 226, Mrs. T. Sewell; 227, Mrs. R. Soule; 228, Miss Emily D. Stebbins; 229, Miss Fanny Steele; 230, Mrs. C. H. Stowell; 231, Mrs. J. T. Sunderland; 232, Mrs. J. H. Wade; 233, Miss Stella Wagner; 234, Mrs. Wm. Waldron; 235, Mrs. C. K. Wead; 236, Miss Lillian Wells; 237, Miss Clara Wheeler; 238, Mrs. J. M. Wheeler; 239, Mrs. A. Winchell; 240, Miss Ida B. Winchell; 241, Mrs. A. B. Wood; 242, Miss Jessie Wood.

NOTICES OF THE LOCAL COMMITTEE.

THURSDAY, AUG. 27.

For the convenience of the Local Committee the programme for the Ann Arbor meeting is to be issued in two parts, and the attention of members is here especially called to this fact.

Members of the Association are requested to register their names at the office of the Local Committee, Room B, University Hall, first floor, as soon as possible after their arrival in the city. Registry blanks are provided for this purpose. Members will register each member of their family on separate blanks. [See programme, Part One, page 18.] A badge will be furnished each person so registered, upon which will be stamped the number attached to the name in the daily printed list of arrivals. These badges are to be worn during the meeting in order to facilitate the arrangements of the Local Committee. Each person provided with a badge will be furnished with a map of the city and such other circulars and notices as may be provided.

Members of the Local Committee will be in attendance, and will be designated by a light blue ribbon marked "Local Committee," and numbered to correspond with the numbers attached to the names, as given on page 6 of this programme. Members of sub-committees will give such information on the subjects of which they have charge as may be desired. The office of the sub-committee on Hotels and Lodgings is in the School of Music building, corner of State and Huron streets, where persons will be in attendance to assist members in securing accommodations, and to direct those for whom lodgings have been secured in advance to the places selected for them.

The office of the Committee on Excursions will be in the room of the Steward of the University, on the first floor of University Hall.

Conversation rooms for ladies and gentlemen will be open on the first floor of the north wing of University Hall.

The representatives of the press will be provided with a special "Press" badge on white ribbon.

In order to secure accuracy authors are requested to furnish reporters with abstracts of their papers.

All botanists, members of the Association, are requested, as soon as they receive their Association badge and number, to register, as members of the Botanical Club, on special blanks provided at the desk of the Local Committee, and to see that their names are entered in a special register kept open for that purpose. They will also receive in addition to the Association badges yellow ribbon to distinguish them as members of the Botanical Club.

For the convenience of those attending the meetings arrangements have been made with a competent caterer to furnish meals—breakfast from 7 to 9, dinner from 12½ to 2, and supper from 6 to 8—at the uniform price of fifty cents each meal, at the "Central Dining Room," in one of the University buildings on the north side of the Campus. Meal tickets can be obtained at the door of the Dining Room.

On Thursday evening, August 27, from 8 to 11 o'clock, the members of the Association will be tendered a reception by the citizens of Ann Arbor at the Court House, corner of Main and Huron Streets. Members of the Association and members of the Local Committee will be admitted on exhibiting their appropriate badges at the door. Other invited guests will be provided with tickets of admission, which must be shown at the door. The sub-committee on invitations to this reception consists of President Angell, Judge Cooley, and Judge Harriman.

On Friday afternoon, from 5 to 7 o'clock, the members of the Association are invited to a Lawn Party to be given on the University Campus, under direction of the Local Committee.

Persons not members of the Association, but who have come to Ann Arbor to attend the meetings, are requested to register their names on arrival at the office of the *Local Committee* in a special book provided for them. By so registering, persons not members of the Association who are provided with the proper railroad certificate, can secure the Local Secretary's signature which will enable them to avail themselves of *reduced rates* on the railroads for their return home. *The Local Secretary will not sign return certificates except for persons whose names are registered with the Local Committee.*

EXCURSIONS.

The Committee on Excursions make the following announcements:

1. The Excursion to the Saginaw Valley, announced in the first circular of the Local Committee, had to be abandoned in consequence of a general and prolonged "strike" among the laborers of the valley.

2. By invitation of citizens of Detroit, an excursion will be made on Saturday, August 29th, "to Detroit; and from there—by boat,—to the Rock Salt Wells, at Marine City, and to the Oakland Summer Resort on the St. Clair River." Dinner will be served at the Oakland House, and a lunch on the steamer during the return. The excursion is entirely free of expense to those entitled to participate. The following is the programme arranged:

A special train of seven coaches, will leave Ann Arbor at 7 a. m., Standard Time, reaching Detroit at 8:15 a. m. The Steamer will leave the Michigan Central R. R. Dock at 8:45 passing the government improvements in Lake St. Clair, and arriving at Marine City at 12:15 p. m. Mr. McElroy, the proprietor of a large salt manufactory, will be prepared to receive the Excursion, and will have his works on exhibition. The Excursion will leave Marine City at 1:15 p. m., arriving at the Oakland House, St. Clair, at 2 p. m., where the dinner will be served.

At 3:30 the Excursion will leave St. Clair on the return. Lunch will be served on the Steamer and Detroit will be reached at 7 p. m.

At 7:30 the train will start for Ann Arbor, arriving about 8:45.

(Detroit time is 30 minutes faster than Central Standard Time, and Ann Arbor time about 27 minutes faster.)

Free tickets, not transferable, and good for the round trip, will be issued to Members and Associate Members and invited guests of the Association, at headquarters of the Excursion Committee, to all bearing the Association Badge. Applications should be made as early as possible after the opening of the Session of the Association. None admitted to the train without tickets.

3. An excursion has been arranged for Wednesday, September 2d, to Mackinac Island; and subordinate excursions from Mackinac to Petoskey, to the Sault Ste. Marie and to Marquette in the Iron Region of Lake Superior. Those participating in this Excursion may return directly from Mackinac or prolong their visit there or on any of the side excursions, and return to Detroit, at their convenience, at any time during the season. This is not a free excursion; but fares and hotel charges have been specially reduced.

Further details are not necessary here, as a circular has been prepared giving all necessary information; and this may be had by early application at headquarters of the Excursion Committee. Members are also referred to the pamphlet accompanying the first circular of the Local Committee. Tickets should be purchased at as early a date as possible after the opening of the Session, in order that all proper arrangements may be made. Tickets will be on sale at the headquarters of the Committee and also on the Steamer during the Excursion of Saturday.

The privileges of this excursion are extended also to the members of the Local Committee and to all persons giving free entertainment to the members and associate members of the Association, and its invited guests.

BOTANICAL CLUB. An afternoon excursion, to occur on Monday, will be given by carriages to the Tamarack Swamp, one of the most interesting localities in the vicinity of Ann Arbor. This is one of the detached spots, common in Southern Michigan, where a northern flora has lingered under favorable conditions through the various climatic changes of later geological times. Various northern Orchids, Coptis, Trientalis, Lycopods, and other interesting plants are found here.

By starting promptly at 2 P. M., an hour and a half can be secured for botanizing, and the party can return to town in time for tea. This excursion will be provided, free of expense, for members of the Association, who are also members of the Botanical Club.

The members of the Botanical Club who intend to make this excursion will please leave their names as early as convenient at the office of the local secretary.

J. C. ARTHUR,
Secretary Botanical Club.

REGISTER OF MEMBERS IN ATTENDANCE.

To 4:30 P. M., Tuesday, August 25.

1. J. P. Lesley, Philadelphia, Pa. Mr. Gordon's, 8 University Ave.
2. H. A. Newton, New Haven, Conn. Mr. Douglas's, [illegible] University Ave.
3. F. W. Putnam, Cambridge, Mass. Corner of State and Huron Streets.
4. Ellen Putnam, Cambridge, Mass. Corner of State and Huron Streets.
5. Miss C. A. Walker, Salem, Mass. [illegible] Ingalls St.
6. Alexander Winchell, Ann Arbor, Mich. N. University Ave.
7. Amos W. Butler, Brookville, Ind. Cor. Thompson and Jefferson Sts.
8. John W. Langley, Ann Arbor, Mich. Washtenaw Ave.
9. W. H. Walmsley, Philadelphia, Pa. [illegible] Division St.
10. T. B. Stowell, Cortland, N. Y. [illegible] University Ave.
11. T. J. Burrill, Champaign, Ill. [illegible] Division St.
12. S. M. Tracy, Columbia, Mo. [illegible] Thompson St.
13. A. B. Prescott, Ann Arbor, Mich. [illegible] Ingalls St.
14. Simon H. Gage, Ithaca, N. Y. 7 N. University Ave.
15. Mrs. Susanna H. Gage, Ithaca, N. Y. 7 N. University Ave.
16. F. A. Gulley, Prof. Agriculture, Agricultural College Mississippi. [illegible] Thompson St.
17. Thomas Taylor, M. D., Microscopist, U. S. Department of Agriculture, Washington, D. C. Mrs. Clements, [illegible] Washtenaw Ave.
18. W. J. Beal, Ingham Co., Mich.; with Dr. J. H. Rivers.
19. Chas K. [illegible], Ann Arbor, Mich. [illegible] Thayer St.
20. W. H. Pettee, Ann Arbor, Mich. [illegible] Thompson St.
21. M. E. Cooley, Ann Arbor, Mich. [illegible] Street.
22. C. J. H. Woodbury, Boston, Mass. Mrs. Fisher's, [illegible] N. University Ave.
23. H. W. Bourne, Providence, R. I. Mrs. Fisher's, [illegible] N. University Ave.
24. C. E. Bessey, Lincoln, Neb. Cor. State and Huron.
25. Dan'l Humphrey, Lawrence, Mass. Judge Page's, [illegible] 12th St.
26. Mrs. E. D. Humphrey, Lawrence, Mass. Judge Page's.
27. E. L. Sturtevant, Geneva, N. Y. [illegible] N. University Ave.
28. Henry E. Alvord, Mountainville, N. Y. [illegible] N. University Ave.
29. J. M. Coulter, Crawfordsville, Ind. Philip Bach's.
30. N. H. Winchell, Minneapolis, Minn. Prof. Winchell's.
31. H. V. Winchell, Minneapolis, Minn. Prof. Winchell's.
32. A. L. Green, Ann Arbor. [illegible] Lawrence St.
33. C. K. Wead, Ann Arbor. [illegible] E. Washington St.
34. R. B. Warder, Lafayette, Ind. Mrs. Becker's.
35. Mrs. R. B. Warder, Lafayette, Ind. Mrs. Becker's.
36. Albert Osborn, Ames, Iowa. [illegible] Jefferson St.
37. Byron D. Halsted, Ames, Iowa. [illegible] Jefferson St.

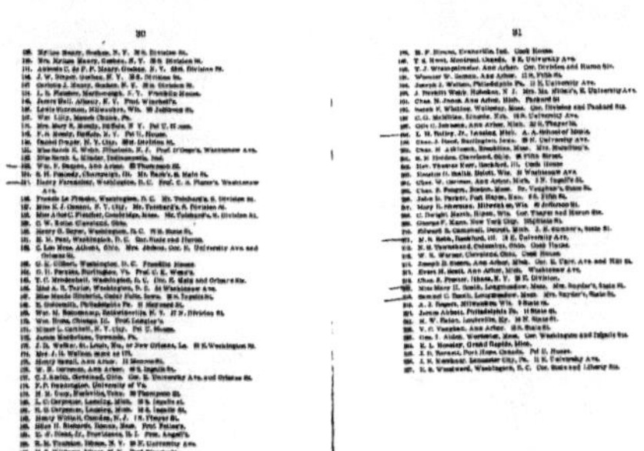

LIST OF NEW MEMBERS ELECTED.

Wednesday, Aug 26.

1. Charles Francis Adams, Detroit, Mich.
2. Charles Heath Atkinson, Brookline, Mass.
3. Prof. Liberty A. Bailey, Jr., Agricultural College, Mich.
4. John Davis Barnett, Port Hope, Ontario, Canada.
5. Rev. William N. [illegible], [illegible], N. Y.
6. M. S. Bebb, Rockford, Ill.
7. Prof. Wooster W. Beman, Ann Arbor, Mich.
8. Rev. Raphael Benjamin, [illegible] Hotel, Cincinnati, Ohio.
9. William Herbert Bixby, Capt. Engineers, U. S. A., Wilmington, N. C.
10. Miss Mary A. Booth, Longmeadow, Mass.
11. Samuel C. Booth, Longmeadow, Mass.
12. Robert W. Bourne, Box [illegible], Providence, R. I.
13. William Bouton, C. E., [illegible] Park Ave., St. Louis, Mo.
14. Douglas H. Campbell, [illegible] Alfred St., Detroit, Mich.
15. Edward D. Campbell, [illegible] Alfred St., Detroit, Mich.
16. H. [illegible] Clayton, Ann Arbor, Mich.
17. Capt. Elmer Lawrence Corthell, [illegible] Nassau St., New York City.
18. Arnold Guyot Dana, New Haven, Ct.
19. Seth Dean, Glenwood, Iowa.
20. Prof. William Henry Dorrance, Ann Arbor, Mich.
21. Harlow A. Douglass, [illegible] St., Chicago, Ill.
22. Henry William [illegible], C. E., [illegible], Pa.
23. Charles E. Emery, Consulting Engr., U. S. Marine, [illegible] Cortlandt St., New York City.
24. L. J. [illegible], M. D., Baker City, Oregon.
25. Leonard Brewer [illegible], Auditor General's Office, Harrisburg, Pa.
26. Charles S. Fellows, [illegible] St., Chicago, Ill.
27. Richard Samuel Floyd, President of the James Lick Trustees, San Francisco, Cal.
28. Thomas E. Fraser, Supt. of the construction of Lick Observatory, Mount Hamilton, San Jose, Cal.
29. Levi Knight Fuller, Brattleboro, Vermont.
30. Charles H. Gibson, [illegible] Clark St., Chicago, Ill.
31. Prof. Le Roy F. Griffin, Lake Forest, Ill.
32. Prof. Louis [illegible], Ph. D., Norwich University, Northfield, Vt.
33. Lt. [illegible] D. Harris, U. S. N., Navy Yard, Mare Island, Cal.
34. William Cleveland Hicks, [illegible] Park Place, New York City.
35. Prof. William Hoover, Athens, Ohio.
36. William Hoskins, [illegible] South Clark St., Chicago.
37. Prof. Charles S. Howe, Akron, Ohio.
38. Hon. John W. Hoyt, Cheyenne, Wyoming Ter.
39. Prof. Otis C. Johnson, Ann Arbor, Mich.
40. Prof. Charles F. Jones, Ann Arbor, Mich.
41. Frank S. Kedzie, Agricultural College, Mich.
42. Miss Nellie S. Kedzie, Kansas Agricultural College Manhattan, Kansas.
43. Joshua Allen Lippincott, President State University, Lawrence, Kas.
44. William A. [illegible], Flint, Mich.
45. James B. [illegible], [illegible], Ill.
46. Dr. J. H. Oyster, Paola, Kansas.
47. Prof. Charles Philip [illegible], [illegible], Mich.
48. Charles [illegible], [illegible], Ohio.
49. J. J. [illegible], [illegible] Indiana Ave., Chicago, Ill.
50. J. H. [illegible], Green Bay, Wis.
51. [illegible] H. [illegible], Ann Arbor, Mich.
52. Horace [illegible], M. D., [illegible] Spruce Street, Philadelphia, Pa.
53. Francis C. Sessions, Columbus, Ohio.
54. Prof. Henry Sewall, Ann Arbor, Mich.
55. Prof. Joseph B. Steere, Ann Arbor, Mich.
56. Prof. Alfred Alexander Titsworth, Alfred Centre, N. Y.
57. Henry Ward Turner, U. S. Geol. Survey, San Francisco, Cal.
58. Prof. Victor C. Vaughan, Ann Arbor, Mich.
59. Frank C. Wagner, Ann Arbor, Mich.
60. Ann Coolidge Warren, [illegible] West [illegible] St., New York City.
61. Miss Lillie E. Warren, [illegible] West [illegible] St., New York City.
62. James N. Warrington, Vulcan Iron Works, Chicago, Ill.
63. Charles H. White, Surgeon U. S. N., Museum of Hygiene, Washington, D. C.
64. Horace V. Winchell, Geol. Survey of Minn., Minneapolis, Minn.
65. Alvinus B. Wood, Ann Arbor, Mich.
66. Theodore J. Wrampelmeier, Ann Arbor, Mich.
67. Walter C. Wyman, [illegible] Dearborn St., Chicago, Ill.
68. Charles Whitney [illegible], [illegible] Ingalls St., Ann Arbor, Mich.
69. Charles L. [illegible], Ann Arbor, Mich.
70. William H. [illegible], Ann Arbor, Mich.
71. Thomas G. Lee, [illegible] Plymouth Ave., Rochester, N. Y.
72. Conway G. MacMillan, Lincoln, Neb.
73. Mrs. Ada [illegible], [illegible] Vine St., Cincinnati, O.
74. Julius [illegible], [illegible] Duane St., New York.
75. James [illegible], [illegible] Locust St., Philadelphia, Pa.
76. Thomas [illegible], M. D., Rockford, Ill.
77. Charles J. [illegible], Burlington, Iowa.
78. A. J. Rogers, [illegible] Warren Ave., Milwaukee, Wis.
79. Prof. J. D. Parker, Chaplain U. S. A., Fort [illegible], Kansas.
80. Prof. Charles Dwight Marsh, Ripon, Wis.
81. Prof. Erastus G. Smith, Beloit, Wis.
82. Edwin L. Moseley, Grand Rapids, Mich.

Ann Arbor, Mich. Aug. 27, '8[illegible]

My dear Deane:

I am having a glorious time. On the register in this pamphlet I have marked most of the members of the Botanical Club present. It is pleasant to meet the botanists — and, in fact, all scientists. You get new impulses and new ideas. How I wish you were here! I go home to-morrow night.

Coulter now has my [illegible] ready for me. I was especially pleased to meet Coulter, having seen most of the botanists before.

Shall expect a letter from you when I get home.

A. F. Warner goes to Cambridge in a month. I told him to be sure to make your acquaintance.

188. H. F. Blount, Evansville, Ind. Cook House.
189. T. S. Hunt, Montreal, Canada. 3 E. University Ave.
190. T. J. Wrampelmeier, Ann Arbor. Cor. Division and Huron Sts.
191. Wooster W. Beman, Ann Arbor. 11 S. Fifth St.
192. Joseph J. Walton, Philadelphia Pa. 11 E. University Ave.
193. J. Burkitt Webb, Hoboken, N. J. Mrs. Mc Millan's, E. University Ave.
194. Chas. N. Jones, Ann Arbor, Mich. Packard St.
195. Sarah F. Whiting, Wellesley, Mass. Cor. Division and Packard Sts.
196. C. G. McMillan, Lincoln, Neb. 16 S. University Ave.
197. Otis C. Johnson, Ann Arbor, Mich. 52 S. Thayer St.
198. L. H. Bailey, Jr., Lansing, Mich. A. A. School of Music.
199. Chas. J. Reed, Burlington, Iowa. 25 N. University Ave.
200. Chas. H. Atkinson, Brookline, Mass. Mrs. Hamilton's.
201. S. E. Holden, Cleveland, Ohio. 20 Fifth Street.
202. Rev. Thomas Kerr, Rockford, Ill. Cook House
203. Erastus G. Smith, Beloit Wis. 51 Washtenaw Ave.
204. Chas. W. Carman, Ann Arbor, Mich. 5 N. Ingalls St.
205. Chas. P. Pengra, Boston, Mass. Dr. Vaughan's, State St.
206. John D. Parker, Fort Hayes, Kan. 9 S. Fifth St.
207. Mary R. Sherman, Milwaukee, Wis. 80 Jefferson St.
208. C. Dwight Marsh, Ripon. Wis. Cor. Thayer and Huron Sts.
209. George F. Kunz, New York City. 10½ State St.
210. Edward D. Campbell, Detroit. Mich. J. E. Sumner's, State St.
211. M. S. Bebb, Rockford, Ill. 13 E. University Ave.
212. N. S. Townshend, Columbus, Ohio. Cook House.
213. W. R. Warner, Cleveland, Ohio. Cook House.
214. Joseph B. Steere, Ann Arbor, Mich. Cor. E. Univ. Ave. and Hill St.
215. Evart H. Scott, Ann Arbor, Mich. Washtenaw Ave.
216. Chas. S. Prosser, Ithaca, N. Y. 28 S. Division.
217. Miss Mary H. Booth, Longmeadow, Mass. Mrs. Snyder's, State St.
218. Samuel C. Booth, Longmeadow, Mass. Mrs. Snyder's, State St.
219. A. J. Rogers, Milwaukee, Wis. 9 State St.
220. James Abbott, Philadelphia Pa. 14 State St.
221. H. W. Eaton, Louisville, Ky. 10 N. State St.
222. V. C. Vaughan, Ann Arbor. 15 S. State St.
223. Geo. I. Alden, Worcester, Mass. Cor. Washington and Ingalls Sts.
224. E. L. Moseley, Grand Rapids, Mich.
225. J. D. Barnett, Port Hope, Canada. Psi U. House.
226. J. E. Kershner, Lancaster City, Pa. 11 E. University Ave.
227. R. S. Woodward, Washington, D. C. Cor. State and Liberty Sts.

To 5:30 P. M. Thursday, Aug. 27.

228. H. H. Clayton, Readville, Mass. Observatory.
229. Alex. Hogg, Fort Worth, Texas.
230. Charles Schäffer, Philadelphia, Pa. Franklin House.
231. Chas. Reemelin, Cincinnati, Ohio. Mrs. Button's, Thompson St.
232. F. C. Wagner, Ann Arbor, Mich. 2 Packard St.
233. E. B. Elliott, Washington, D. C. Cook House.
234. Miss L. A. Elliott, Washington, D. C. Cook House.
235. W. A. Locy, Flint, Mich. 27 Thompson St.

236. Chas. Francis, Detroit, Mich. 87 E. Washington St.
237. Morris B. Belknap, Louisville, Ky. Cor. William and Division Sts.
238. O. S. Westcott, Maywood, Ill. Cook House.
239. Joseph Libbey, Georgetown, D. C. Mrs. Swathell's, State St.
240. W. L. Coffinberry, Grand Rapids. Cor. Jefferson and Thompson Sts.
241. C. W. Rolfe, Urbana, Ill.
242. P. J. Farnsworth, Clinton, Iowa. Cor. Liberty and State Sts.
243. Mrs. P. J. Farnsworth, Clinton, Iowa. Cor. Liberty and State Sts.
244. C. G. Wheeler, Chicago. 10½ State st.
245. C. F. Mabery, Cleveland, Ohio. Cook House.
246. T. D. Robertson, Rockford, Ill. Mrs. Truesdale's, S. University Ave.
247. Mrs. S. A. Robertson, Rockford, Ill. Mrs. Truesdale's, S. University Ave.
248. E. M. Colburn, Peoria, Ill. Mrs. Child's, Maynard St.
249. D. H. Campbell, Detroit, Mich. J. E. Sumner's.
250. J. A. Brashear, Pittsburgh, Pa. 20 Division St.
251. Mrs. J. A. Brashear, Pittsburgh, Pa. 20 Division St.
252. M. H. Crump, Bowling Green, Ky. 79 E. Ann St.
253. F. C. Sessions, Columbus, Ohio, J. Q. A. Sessions.
254. H. F. Walling, Cambridge, Mass.
255. W. Z. Bennett, Wooster, Ohio. Mr. Williams', Jefferson St.
256. Mrs. Minnie S. Bennett, Wooster, Ohio. Mrs. Williams', Jefferson St.
257. Ada Merrill, Cincinnati, Ohio. Mr. Worden's, William St.
258. S. P. Langley, Allegheny, Pa. Prof. J. W. Langley's.
259. H. W. Wiley, Washington, D. C. Cook House.
260. A. G. Clark, Cambridgeport, Mass. Dr. Jackson's.
261. Malcolm McNeil, Princeton, N. J. 65 E. Division St.
262. Josephine Murtfeldt, Kirkwood, Mo. 74 S. State St.
263. J. H. Norton, Ravenswood, Ill. 36 S. Division St.
264. Mrs. J. H. Norton, Ravenswood, Ill. 36 S. Division St.
265. Lucia E. Blount, Evansville, Ind. Cook House.
266. J. H. Kedzie, Evanston, Ill. 26 S. Division St.
267. L. H. Trowbridge, Detroit, Mich. 20 William St.
268. Mrs. L. H. Trowbridge, Detroit, Mich. 20 William St.
269. Charles S. Clarke, Peoria, Ill. Mrs. Childs', Maynard St.
270. A. V. E. Young, Boston, Mass. Dr. A. B. Prescott's.
271. J. L. Campbell, Crawfordsville, Ind. Cook House.
272. J. N. Stockwell, Cleveland, Ohio. Mrs. Gibhart's, S. University Ave.
273. H. W. Smith, St. Paul, Minn.
274. G. B. Richmond, Detroit, Mich.
275. C. S. Peirce, N. Y. City. Ten Brook House.
276. Mrs. C. S. Peirce, N. Y. City. Ten Brook House.
277. A. Macfarlane, Austin, Texas. 18 Ingalls St.
278. J. F. James, Cincinnati, Ohio.
279. J. M. Schaeberle, Ann Arbor, Mich. Observatory.
280. D. S. Owens, Franklin, Ind.
281. Delos Fall, Albion, Mich. 20 Thompson St.
282. J. F. McElroy, Lansing, Mich. Cor. Division and Washington Sts.
283. Lewis McLouth, Ypsilanti, Mich.
284. H. B. Baker, Lansing, Mich. Mr. Clarkson's, Fifth St.
285. L. D. Watkins, Manchester, Mich. Mr. Clarkson's, Fifth St.
286. F. L. Scribner, Washington, D. C. 25 Thompson St.

287. J. H. Kellogg, Battle Creek, Mich. Cook House.
288. W. H. Lennon, Brockport, N. Y. 35 S. Division St.
289. Henry Gillman, Detroit, Mich.
290. G. W. Hubbard, Nashville, Tenn. Philip Bach's, Main St.
291. E. F. Smith, Lansing, Mich. Mrs. Graves', Catherine St.
292. C. F. Wheeler, Hubbardston, Mich. Cor. Division and Washington Sts.
293. Jno. Müller, Ann Arbor. 97 E Huron St.
294. M. L. Rouse, Toronto, Canada. Franklin House.
295. C. E. Slocum, Defiance, Ohio. 54 E. Washington St.
296. A. J. Baker, Ann Arbor, Mich. 46 E. William St.
297. Mrs. A. M. S. Sawyers, Groesbeck, Texas. 85 E. Washington St.
298. H. N. Chute, Ann Arbor, Mich. 14 S. Thayer St.
299. Miss Jennie C. Newton, Norwich, N. Y. 14 S. University Ave.
300. O. Cinte, Iowa City, Iowa. Rev. J. T. Sunderland's.
301. O. W. Wight, Detroit, Mich. Detroit, Mich.
302. V. M. Spalding, Ann Arbor, Mich. S, Ingalls and Monroe Sts.
303. W. L. Hooper, College Hill, Mass. 36 Ingalls St.
304. Howard Ayers, Ann Arbor, Mich. 27 Thompson St.
305. J. H. Pillsbury, Northampton, Mass. Mr. Truesdale's, S. Univ. Ave.
306. E. C. Hogeboom, Shelbyville, Ky. 30 Jefferson St.
307. Henry Gradle Chicago, Ill. Dr. Lupinski's.
308. S. H. Culver, Mason, Mich. 18 Maynard St.
309. H. S. Williams, Charles City, Iowa. 8 N. State St.
310. J. G. White. Lincoln, Neb. Cook House.
311. Chas. F. Scott, Columbus, Ohio. C. Boylan's, Division St.

LIST OF NEW MEMBERS ELECTED.

Wednesday, Aug. 26.

1. Charles Francis Adams, Detroit, Mich.
2. Charles Heath Atkinson, Brookline, Mass.
3. Prof. Liberty A. Bailey, Jr., Agricultural College, Mich.
4. John Davis Barnett, Port Hope, Ontario, Canada.
5. Rev. William N. Beauchamp, Baldwinsville, N. Y.
6. M. S. Bebb, Rockford, Ill.
7. Prof. Wooster W. Beman, Ann Arbor, Mich.
8. Rev. Raphael Benjamin, Hexter's Hotel, Cincinnati, Ohio.
9. William Herbert Bixby, Capt. Engineers, U. S. A., Wilmington, N. C.
10. Miss Mary A. Booth, Longmeadow, Mass.
11. Samuel C. Booth, Longmeadow, Mass.
12. Robert W. Bourne, Box 217, Providence, R. I.
13. William Bouton, C. E., 2909 Park Ave., St. Louis, Mo.
14. Douglas H. Campbell, 91 Alfred St., Detroit, Mich.
15. Edward D. Campbell, 91 Alfred St., Detroit, Mich.
16. H. Helm Clayton, Ann Arbor, Mich.
17. Capt. Elmer Lawrence Corthell, 31 Nassau St., New York City.
18. Arnold Guyot Dana, New Haven, Ct.
19. Seth Dean, Glenwood, Iowa.
20. Prof. William Henry Dorrance, Ann Arbor, Mich.
21. Gayton A. Douglass, 229 State St., Chicago, Ill.
22. Henry William Dunne, C. E., Bryn Mawr, Pa.
23. Charles E. Emery, Consulting Engr., U. S. Marine, 22 Cortlandt St., New York City.
24. L. J. Estes, M. D., Baker City, Oregon.
25. Leonard Bertner Eyster, Auditor General's Office, Harrisburg, Pa.
26. Charles S. Fellows, 38 Throop St., Chicago, Ill.
27. Richard Samuel Floyd, President of the James Lick Trustees, San Francisco, Cal.
28. Thomas E. Fraser, Supt. of the construction of Lick Observatory, Mount Hamilton, San Jose, Cal.
29. Levi Knight Fuller, Brattleboro, Vermont.
30. Charles H. Gibson, 81 Clark St., Chicago, Ill.
31. Prof. La Roy F. Griffin, Lake Forest, Ill.
32. Prof. Louis Habel, Ph. D., Norwich University, Northfield, Vt.
33. Lt. Uriah R. Harris, U. S. N., Navy Yard, Mare Island, Cal.
34. William Cleveland Hicks, 19 Park Place, New York City.
35. Prof. William Hoover, Athens, Ohio.
36. William Hoskins, 81 South Clark St., Chicago.
37. Prof. Charles S. Howe, Akron, Ohio.

Aug. 31, 1885

My Dear Deane: Had a good time at Ann Arbor. Several other botanists came after I wrote you from there. I enclose a list of them.

Your No. 45 is Carex tentaculata typica

No. 46 C. lupulina typica

I am much interested in your notes on Vaccinium. Shall put the fruit on ice as soon as it comes.

Begin daily lectures next Thursday.

I am now reading my Carex proof for Coulter's Manual.

so loaded before.

Prof. J. C. Arthur is coming here to stay a few days with me.

Regards to Mrs. D.

In a hurry,

L. H. B. Jr.

Sweet's Hotel.
N.C. JOHNSON PROPRIETOR.
Grand Rapids, Mich.
Sept. 10 1885

My Dear Deane:

This is a most beautiful city. I have been here 2 or 3 times before, but never saw so much of the little city as now. It is a neat and compact city of 50,000 people, a city of the most magnificent dwellings I ever saw.

I am of course busy with my exhibit and with noted pomologists. I enclose you a list of the fruits I have on exhibition. My display attracts the most attention of any in the Hall. The Vacciniums are especially fine. To-morrow we leave the "Valley City" and go to my own home to spend Sunday. We return to College next Monday.

I suppose that you are now having a good time in Nantucket.

Yours hastily
L. H. Bailey, Jr.

I have written Mr. Churchill thanking him for the grapes.

DEPARTMENT OF
HORTICULTURE AND LANDSCAPE
GARDENING,

Agricultural College, Mich., Sept. 15. 1885

My Dear Deane: We arrived home last night. Had a good time. I was awarded a bronze medal for my wild fruits. I was asked to put in a bill of my expenses, and not having heard from you I could not put in your bill. Glad you have a good time at Nantucket. Yours L. H. B. Jr.

Walter Deane,
Brewster Place,
Cambridge, Mass.

American Pomological Society.

Michigan Exhibit.

1885.

Grower, ……………………………………

Residence, ……………

American Pomological Society.

Michigan Exhibit.

1885.

Grower, ...

Residence, ...

[illegible]

[illegible]

[illegible]

Cra[illegible]

[illegible]

Corylus rostr[illegible]

C. Ame[illegible]

Oak apple [illegible]

Diospyros Virg

Carpinus [illegible]

American Pomological Society.

Michigan Exhibit.

1885.

Grower, ...

Residence, ...

Carya porcina
— olivaefor
C. alba
Celtis
Fagus ferru
Juglans nig
[illegible]
Platanus
Liriodendron
Ptelea

American Pomological Society.

Michigan Exhibit.

1885.

Grower, ...

Residence, ...

American Pomological Society.

Michigan Exhibit.

1885.

Grower, ...

Residence, ...

Nemopanthes [illegible]
Smilax rotund[illegible]
Cornus seri[illegible]
[illegible] paniculata [illegible]
Rhus typhina
Xanthoxylum A[illegible]
Symphoricarpos [illegible]
[illegible] [illegible]
Sarra[illegible]

American Pomological Society.

Michigan Exhibit.

1885.

Grower, ...

Residence, ...

Thuja o[illegible]ta
Clematis [illegible]
Staphylea
Pinus Strobus
Abies Ex[illegible]a
Xanthium Ca[illegible]
Smilacina [illegible]
Cypripedium a[illegible]

American Pomological Society.

Michigan Exhibit.

1885.

Grower, ...

Residence, ...

American Pomological Society.

Michigan Exhibit.

1885.

Grower, ...

Residence, ...

F. collina

F. elator

F. virg. v.

880

American Pomological Society.

Michigan Exhibit.

1885.

Grower, ...

Residence, ...

My Dear Deane:

By this time you are probably returned from Ashland and from a pleasant visit with Mr. Manning. You must have had a pleasant summer.

Here is one of your cards, dated Sept. 4, and I find that I have not answered it. There is no such Carex as C. echinata var. alpicola. If I wrote it that way I made a slip. Var. alpicola belongs to C. canescens (see Suppl. Carex Cat.) It is var. vitilis of Manual. Var. scirpoides of the Manual is now var. microcarpa of C. echinata.

In my list the "Carex straminea forma (C. foenea var. ferruginea)" is simply C. straminea. I have not yet decided whether the form is distinct enough for a variety. It is the C. foenea var.? ferruginea of the Manual.

I have Spiranthes simplex from Ward, but should like a specimen or two from you also.

Have been again to the cold swamp where I found Habenaria ciliaris and what do you suppose I found! — Carex pauciflora!! This is undoubtedly the most southern locality known. See Cat. of Mich. Plants.

You certainly did well at Nantucket. Should have

Oh Yes, your Vacciniums kept nicely and they are still in perfect order! On returning from Grand Rapids I put them in a preserving fluid so that I can have them to illustrate my lectures on wild fruits. Years hence, when you visit me, you shall find them as fresh as when you picked them on New Hampshire hills.

The Carex from Nantucket is Tentaculata. I hope you secured Quercus illicifolia & Q. prinoides for me.

This is beautiful weather — warm, clear & ruddy. It is the hale old age of the year.

Let me hear from you often.

Yours as ever,
L. H. Bailey, Jr.

My Dear Deane:

How I wish I had known that you want Solidago stricta! It is not marked on your list. The swamps are full of it. Shall try to get it yet. If I do not will send you a duplicate which I have but it is poor.

Yes, Lloyd's Carex collected June 8, 1883, at Cincinnati is cristata v. mirabilis. So are the plants from Willoughby which I so named. The specimens differ much in color, but not so much in other characters. His grew in shade and yours in sun. Moreover, yours approach cristata itself and also the northern form of lagopodioides (v. moniliformis). I am nearly convinced that the only proper disposition of v. mirabilis is to give it up entirely, throwing it into cristata, lagopodioides and straminea. It has no characters which are not contained in one or the other of those species. It is thoroughly an intermediate form, and therefore variable and highly perplexing.

Your no. 19 is C. echinata Murr. v. microcarpa Boeck. (C. stellulata v. scirpoides Kunze)

Many, many thanks for the verification of the

plants.

No, I never got Quercus ilicifolia

I never found Solidago Ohioensis, Riddellii nor Houghtonii and am not sure that I have S. patula.

Aster ericoides is abundant, but not the var. villosus;

Never found A. aestivus, azureus, tenuifolius. Have single specimens of all [two] in herb. Lawrence.

Solidago Riddellii grows in Bot. Gardens.

Patterson sent me a photo of Torreys and Grays peaks. He also sent me a full set of the Carices he has collected this summer to name. They are a fine lot. When he sends labels I shall make you a duplicate set, unless you are contemplating purchasing a full set of his Colorado plants.

You are very kind to lay aside so many Nantucket plants for me. I shall appreciate them.

Did you find Aster Herveyi? I am not sure about your Setaria. They are very puzzling. Will give it more attention soon.

Beautiful Indian summer now.

Yours as ever,

L. H. Bailey, jr.

HORTICULTURAL DEPARTMENT,
AGRICULTURAL COLLEGE.

Lansing, Michigan, Sept. 5, 1885

My Dear Deane:

Just time for a line. The box of plants is rec'd with contents as fresh and bright as when they were picked. Please accept my everlasting thanks. Also, be sure to send an item of your expenditure of time and money. Have rec'd a box of grapes from Churchill. Your dried plants also rec'd. Very nice. Thanks. The other day I found in abundance Habenaria ciliaris. Do you want any?

The fruiting spec. of Horse radish is very interesting. It is a great rarity. Never saw it before. Your spec. of Gymnostichum Hystrix is also interesting – it is pubescent. (See Wheeler & Smith's Flora of Michigan)

I go to Grand Rapids next Tuesday. Will be gone there and to my old home a week or so. Have a good time at Nantucket.

Yours &c

My Dear Deane:

I rejoice with you in your nice set of ferns from Mr. Davenport.

Don't be in a hurry about my Nantucket plants.

During my odd minutes I am now arranging and labelling my collections of the summer. What a job it is! And I have a raft of them too; many more than I thought I had. You see, I have put very few in my herb. this summer – have just filed them away in the rough as I took them from the driers. I never collected common things very diligently about here until this summer. What a pleasure it is to know that you have in your herb. all the weeds of the garden and trees of the forest! What a treasure an herbarium is, anyway! Here are all the wonderful and fascinating plants of this interesting region snugly tucked away in my little room up stairs; and next winter when Boreas (excuse the poetry) sweeps down volumes of snow and all

Here are sedges from swamps, and willows and birches from fragrant tangles, and clematis and nettles from exasperating fence-rows; and who would forget the potamogetons and the utricularies and the other oddities which are hidden from common ken?

L. H. Bailey, Jr.

DEPARTMENT OF
HORTICULTURE AND LANDSCAPE
GARDENING,

Agricultural College, Mich., Oct. 5, 1885

Plants arrived. Very nice. Thanks. Cold. More anon.

L. H. B. Jr.

POSTAL CARD.

NOTHING BUT THE ADDRESS CAN BE PLACED ON THIS SIDE.

Walter Deane,
Brewster Place,
Cambridge, Mass.

My Dear Deane:

I can't help it. I have been too busy to write before.

Have looked over your plants. They were very nice. Thanks.

I send you a little parcel by express prepaid. On top you will find a few bitternuts, Carya amara. They are from the same tree as the leaves in the same bundle and picked at the same time. The oak, Q. rubra, numbered 1, is from the same tree from which I once gave you flowers, collected in '78 or '79, under the name of Q. coccinea. In my student days the tree was labelled Q. coccinea, but it is not as you can see at once by fruit. The No. 2, Q. macrocarpa, is from same tree as the flowers I sent you last spring. The same remark applies to 4, Q. alba, and 5, Q. tinctoria. The two labelled 3, Q. bicolor, are from same tree.

Your labiate is evidently some introduced Salvia.

Dr. Gray is changeable in regard to many of those Solidagos. I have had an experience similar to yours.

Met Barnes? Yes, here it is in your letter. Fine fellow.

Oh, so many plants! A big batch of Carices from Oregon — no duplicates — two or three new species. All the Carices of Purdue University to name! And now Mr. Morong has sent all his carices! Three public lectures to write in 2 weeks! A lecture before class every day! and as much more!

Forgot that you wanted me to write names of Carices in ink on sheet, so returned them with a slip on them.

No, var. strictior of C. stricta is n.g. Yes, all ~~are~~ the same, the var. & species — all C. stricta see Bot. Gaz. Sept. '84

Your Panicum dichotomum is the autumnal state which Dr. Gray speaks of, as I understand it.

The Cyperus Nuttallii appears to be correct.

Zannichellia is evidently correct, but it has no fruit.

I find that I made a mistake in my hurry and returned the Carices which you intended me to keep. No matter. I did not need them.

Yours &c

L. H. Bailey, Jr.

Michigan Agricultural College,

HORTICULTURAL DEPARTMENT.

Agricultural College P. O.
Ingham Co., Mich. Nov. 14, 1885

My Dear Deane:

The flower and leaf of Cnicus muticus are from the same plant. The fruits and lvs. of Archangelica hirsuta are also, but those of A. atropurpurea are from different plant.

Montelia tamariscina is what Wheeler's Cat. calls Acnida tuberculata. The names of this plant are constantly changing.

My Quercus Prinus may be the var. acuminata. I can't get any distinctions from Manual description.

The Q. rubra in frt, I sent you this fall is not from the same tree as ~~that in~~ flower I sent you last spring, but it is from the same tree as that young Coccinea of 1880.

What is this that Barnes says about my "Coming out"? I long to hear of the testimonial to Dr. Gray.

Oh, dear! Carex! Carex! Had just got through with Mr. Morong's whole collection, and a batch came from Minnesota. Just got through with that and to-day one came from Dr. Vasey. This last is one of peculiar interest. The plants are from the Louisiana swamps and the Yellowstone River. It contains three plants new to America if not to science. Two of these are from Louisiana. I must have a half dozen new species on hand now.

Next year C. F. Wheeler, Dr. Beal and myself are going to revise the Cat. of Mich. Plants. We are going to make it an economic catalogue as well as scientific. I shall do the economic part. Going to make it the first economic cat. ever published. Dr. Beal and I are also preparing a catalogue of the plants in the vicinity of the College. Will not be published

Michigan Agricultural College,

HORTICULTURAL DEPARTMENT.

Agricultural College P. O.,

Ingham Co., Mich. .... 188....

for a year or more.

I am going to have some herb. cases made this winter. I have collected lots and lots of rubbish this summer. However, I do not collect so many duplicates as I used to.

Should like ever so much to see you and have a good visit.

Let me hear from you.

Yours as ever,

L. H. Bailey, Jr.

My Dear Sir— Dec. 10

[illegible] have been unable to get [illegible]. We move to-day [illegible] 861 Main St., 3 [illegible] [illegible] Baptist Church — near [illegible] [illegible] [illegible]. Will try & get up Sat[illegible] [illegible]. Come [illegible]

[illegible] [illegible] [illegible]

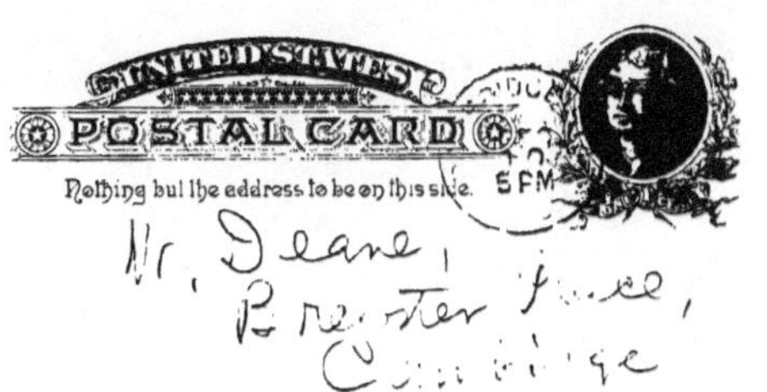
UNITED STATES
POSTAL CARD
Nothing but the address to be on this side.
5 PM
Mr. Deane,

Cambridge, Nov. 27

I have changed my quarters from Linden St. to 12 Wallace — with Mrs. Cleveland. The second house on the left. Call.

L. H. Bailey, Jr.

UNITED STATES
POSTAL CARD
Nothing but the address to be on this side

Friday Dec 18

If you will be at home to-morrow (Saturday) P.M. I will come up at 1 or 2 o'clock.

L. H. B. Jr.

W. Deane,
Brewster Place,
Cambridge Mass

Linnaea Vol. XL p. 337 – C. [illegible]

America's [illegible]

Vol. IV p. 1130 – Tab 419 –

HIBBARD HOUSE.

JACKSON, MICH. [illegible] 188

My dear Dean: We arrived at Lansing in proper order at 5 o'clock Saturday morning. Saturday I visited the College. Found things in good condition. Six of our College men are now off for another Farmer's institute. It begins to-night. Shall not get back to Lansing until next Sunday or Monday.

Shall be very ——— glad to get settled down at home again. Be it ever so far out West there is no place like home.

We had a pleasant trip home except one day in New York. It rained very hard all day there. I saw all of Olney's Carices this time and also all in Herb. Torrey.

Question no. ——— Please look in Linnaea (The vols. stand against the glue room) and see if Boeckeler describes

Carex pedunculata Muhl. and what habitat he gives. His writing on Carex is in vols. 39, 40 & 41, 40 & 41 being bound together, with a good index in the back of each volume. I think that you will find it in vol. 41 if at all. Then look in Boott's big work for C. Baltzellii General index in part IV, and see what habitat he gives, and also what habitat he gives for C. pedunculata. I want especially to know if he saw Drummond[']s spec. [of C. pedunculata] from New Orleans and what number the specimens bore. I am in no hurry for answer.

Regards to Mrs. D. I shall expect a letter from you on my return to Lansing.

Yours ever
[illegible]

Boott Carices.
Vol I p 16.
Ch. Baltzellii –
Hab. In umbrosis [illegible] [illegible]
Florida, Chapman [illegible] [illegible] Tab XLIII

Office of the Secretary.

188.....   To....   Dr.

Please Sign Receipt on the BACK of this Voucher and Return at once.

Agricultural College, Mich.
Feb. 2nd, '86

My Dear Deane:

Your letter containing the Carex note is at hand. It answers the question to my satisfaction. Many Thanks.

Yes, your C. straminea var. chlorostachys is C. foenea Willd. C. straminea var. festucacea is C. straminea.

The two institutes before which I lectured passed off pleasantly. No one was hurt by my lecture.

College opens to-morrow. My [illegible] is sick and so that I am busy. Will write more soon.

Regards [illegible]

Yours as ever,
L. H. Bailey

Paid by Warrant No. ....

Rec'd ....

and .... $\frac{}{100}$ *dollars in full of the within account,* .... *188.*

....

Approved by State Board of Agriculture.

.................................*188*...

....
Chairman of Committee on Accounts.

Michigan Agricultural College,

COLLEGE FACULTY.

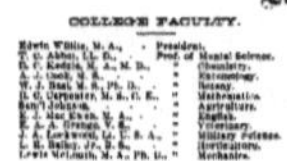

HORTICULTURAL DEPARTMENT.

Agricultural College P. O.,
Ingham Co., Mich. Mar. 8 188[illegible].

Dear Deane:

The Carices from Faxon are all correct. No. 2 included two things, one specimen of C. tenella and two specimens of some undeveloped Vigneae. No. 7 is undoubtedly a hybrid and probably C. debilis × virescens. I send it out will keep this specimen also. Will also keep the C. arcta and one specimen of C. [illegible]. C. arcta becomes C. canescens var. polystachya Boott.

I am now working very hard with a special class of 12 bright seniors in advanced work. Keeps me "humping"!

Excuse this short letter. Will write more when I get time. Hope you are well. Regards to Mrs. D.

Yours Truly,

L. H. Bailey, Jr.

Michigan Agricultural College,

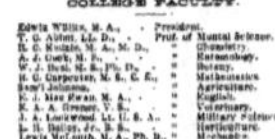

HORTICULTURAL DEPARTMENT.

Agricultural College P.O.
Ingham Co., Mich. Mar. 7 1886

My Dear Dean:

Sunday again and I find a few moments leisure to write to you. I feel like rejoicing over the condition of my herbarium. I saw that you knew it was arranged or rather disarranged. A box which I had fitted up with a door held a part of the plants, the others were spread along on open shelves in the hall where they were always in the way and always catching dirt. A few days ago I got in a new and tight chestnut case containing 45 pigeon holes. I have filled it up. It holds my Carices and my other U.S. plants down to the Cyperaceae. All my old collection are stacked up and disposed in a neat pile. My duplicates have all been placed in the box which before held my specimens. Now things assume a neat appearance in my little room and I am not ashamed to take visitors there. What a comfort

Oh dear! [illegible] losing [illegible] about that [illegible] synopsis. Of course the whole thing must be copying [illegible] [illegible] [illegible] then [illegible] [illegible] [illegible] [illegible] pages since leaving [illegible]! But [illegible] I hope — [illegible] a few weeks rest — to have more time to work on it.

I have nice little class of [illegible]. A dozen [illegible] [illegible] [illegible] — and [illegible] number for [illegible] study in the senior course — [illegible] course — must [illegible] magnificent. For next two weeks I have lectured upon the variation of plants. I divide the subject as follows:

1. Theory of inherent Variation — one lecture [illegible]
2. Variation due to Changes in conditions of life as entertained by Darwin and most [illegible] [illegible]:
   a. Due to increase of ~~food~~ supply.
   b. " " change of latitude and altitude
   c. " " " climate.

Michigan Agricultural College,

HORTICULTURAL DEPARTMENT.

Agricultural College P. O.,
Ingham Co., Mich. 188

a. Due to ~~change~~ cultivation of man.
b. " " selection " "
c. " cross-fertilization.
d. " " and variation
e. " " methods of propagation.

I want this year to grow plants of as many Daturas as possible for purposes of crossing, etc. – now have seeds of D. Tatula and D. inermis. Can you send me any more? Don't care for more than a dozen or so of each.

We are both well and happy. Regards to Mrs. E.

Yours as ever,

L. H. Bailey, Jr.

DEPARTMENT OF HORTICULTURE AND LANDSCAPE GARDENING. Agricultural College, Mich., Mar. 24 1886

My Dear Deane: I will send you a Michigan Farmer which contains the lecture I delivered at our institutes this winter. Nothing new, except abominably bad roads. Have been doing considerable herbarium work of late. Have just got a lot of Cyperaceae from Europe and the vicinity of Australia.

Write. L. H. Bailey, Jr.

Walter Deane,
Brewster Place,
Cambridge,
Mass.

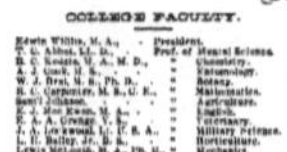

Michigan Agricultural College,

COLLEGE FACULTY.

HORTICULTURAL DEPARTMENT,

Agricultural College P. O.
Ingham Co., Mich. Mch. 3, 1886

My dear Deane:

Yours of the 28th is just at hand. Glad to hear. Did not know that Dr Zuckerman was dead. Sorry to hear that Dr Gray is so bad. I feel anxious about him.

Wish I might have been with you at Mr. Kennedy's. I can imagine how Baines feels over the microscope.

I enclose my lecture.

Don't know where you can find correspondence of Carey and Mead.

Have seen no spring flowers yet.

Don't know that I have any news. Working hard now on Carex synopsis. Dr Gray will advise its publication in Amer. Acad.

Regards to Mrs. D. Drop a line whenever you can. Don't wait for me. Yours &c

L. H. Bailey, Jr.

DEPARTMENT OF
HORTICULTURE AND LANDSCAPE
GARDENING.

Agricultural College, Mich., Apr. 6 1886

My Dear D: I have two references which I would like you to look up for me when you have time: Carex Pacifica, Drejer - look in Boott and see where it was published - Carex Haydenii, Dewey, look in Dewey's Carex (under D.) and find page where it was published - Yours as ever,

Am working hard on Carex. L. H. Bailey, Jr.

POSTAL CARD
MICH.
Walter Deane,
Brewster Place,
Cambridge,
Mass.

My Dear Deane:

Thanks for the Carex notes. They were alright, but you need not have answered them so fully. Still I have two others for you: Look in Torrey's Monogr. of N. Amer. Cyper. and find page where C. Wilkesii is published. You will find the book under T. There are two monographs there side by side, one by Schw. & Torr. and the other – the one I want – by Torrey. Then under W find Wahlenberg's Inledning til Caricographien and find page where he published C. latifolia. I simply want the number of the page ~~in each case~~ Acta Holm. 1803 p. 156. or Inled. p. 108. to make my references complete. Sorry to trouble you so much.

Thanks for the Datura seeds. This work has been repaged in reprinting.

I have now my Carex notes in shape for the printer through 222 species. Some fifty more species.

The bulletin is a very small part of my work. You have no idea of how many things I have on my hands to manage.

Glad that you are coming to Buffalo. We will have a large time. Shall I hope that if you get that—far that you will come home with us?

Regards to Mrs. D.

Yours as ever

L. H. Bailey Jr.

I send you a marked Mich. Hort.

Lots of Hepatica.

My Dear Deane:

By the time this reaches you, you will have returned from your vacation trip. Hope you have had a pleasant time. Things jog along here as usual. Weather unusually fine for this time of year. The Carex MSS. still hangs on. I am now done with 258 species; about 30 more. I am sorry to trouble you with more queries but I see no way of avoiding it. I want references simply.

1. I want to know where Dewey published C. prairea. It is not in the index to his book on Carex; you will have to look in Boott for it. I want simply to know where it was published so ~~that I~~ can cite it as a synonym. Woods Bot. 750 (1861)

2. Find the page in Torrey's Monograph (1836) where he refers to C. dioica L. 387 (now C. gynocrates).

3. Look in Boott and find the page where he describes C. cephaloidea. III. ~~[illegible]~~ 123. pl 395

I have secured the poplars for you.

I was annoyed the other day to have returned to me a letter which I addressed to you at Cambridge, *Mich*. I enclose it as it will be just as good now as when intended. That also contains queries. Hope I am about through bothering you.

Yours truly,

L. H. Bailey, Jr.

My Dear Deane:

Yours of the 6th is at hand. I am under great obligations to you for the replies to my questions and especially for the picture of the natural bridge. You are very kind to think of me on your trips.

The questions were all right, but I would like to have the page and no. of the plate in Botany of the Wilkes Exped. where C. Wilkesii is mentioned.

I am now through with the 288 species of American Carices. I am now to add my bibliography. In a few days my Mss. goes to the printer.

I am glad ~~that~~ you had a good time on your trip. Don't give up going to Buffalo.

Yours as ever,

L. H. Bailey, Jr.

DEPARTMENT OF
HORTICULTURE AND LANDSCAPE
GARDENING.

Agricultural College, Mich. May 23 1886

My Dear Deane:

I know of no reason why it should be very hot in Buffalo in August.

I have made a few changes in Carex names lately. The old C. lagopodioides var. moniliformis becomes C. tribuloides var. reducta. I got rid of this var. moniliformis because I find that Tuckerman's var. moniliformis of C. straminea (var. silicea Bailey) must stand, and two such names for closely related plants would lead to confusion.

We are now in the midst of our week's recess. I took one fine trip with Dr. Beal Friday P.M. into a deep tamarack swamp where the sphagnum sinks far under the pressure of the feet. I waded through rods of Carex utriculata (which I had never seen growing until the day before) in ties and Vaccinium corymbosum almost hid the high tamaracks and Abies nigra overhead. Cypripedium acaule was in elegant flower, and the charming Andromeda polifolia (which I had never seen in flower before) filled me with delight. Menyanthes was there. How delicate are its fringes! And then I found three Carices in excellent condition which I had never seen growing before — C. chordorrhiza, C. Magellanica and C. limosa. On high land near the swamp I found Vaccinium Canadense, which I had never seen growing before. Do you wonder that I enjoyed the tramp?

My career MW. has gone! I feel a sense of relief.

Your article in Current Gazette is fresh and good. Glad you wrote it.

Yours as ever,

L. H. Bailey, Jr.

May 27, 1886

My Dear Deane:

This fall I am going to issue a small set of Carices and I want very much to include C. conoidea and C. vulgaris, two species which I have not yet found here. C. conoidea grows in abundance in the grassy field this side the Cambridge pumping works at Fresh Pond, and in the wet places, near by, the stiff and bluish C. vulgaris is abundant. Can you get me about 15 spec. of each?

Yours truly, L. H. Bailey, Jr.

Walter Deane,
Brewster Place,
Cambridge, Mass.

Yes. I expect that I am authority for Carex tribuloides var. reducta. I don't think of any other change which touches you.

A few days ago I sent Mr. Bebb four willows which puzzled me. One is new. He never saw it before. It is probably some hybrid. It grows in a great swamp near here, a swamp which contains two or three thousand acres. Have looked several times again for the willow, but without success. On a tramp for it yesterday I found Carex aquatilis for the first time — only a single specimen of it, however. I have found about 60 carices just about here, among them C. formosa, the one of all others among manual species which I have had difficulty in securing. Shall lay aside specimens for you. Mr. Bebb volunteered to send me a collection of willows.

I haven't time to make a desiderata list this summer.

Agricultural College, Mich.,
June 5, '86

My Dear D:

Here I am again to trouble you. I want a rough tracing made of one of the ~~large~~ enlarged perigynia of typical laxiflora in Boott's Ill.

I have found the rare willow again. Will save you spec.

Yours &c
L. H. Bailey, Jr.

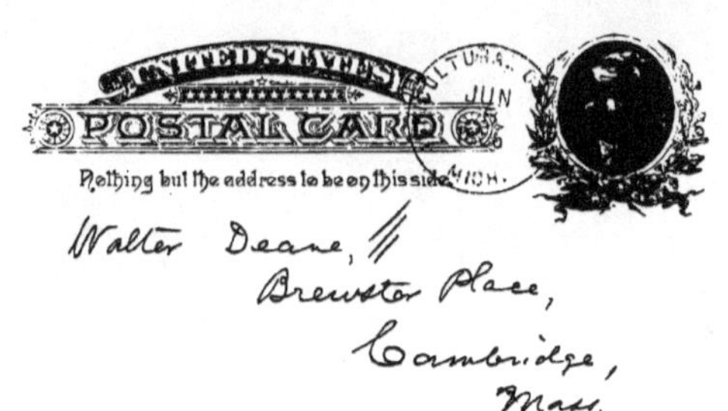

Walter Deane,
Brewster Place,
Cambridge,
Mass.

Agricultural College, Mich.,
June 7, '86.

My Dear Deane:

The sprig you send is Carex stricta. Never mind, I would like to distribute that form of C. stricta as well as C. vulgaris. C. vulgaris does not grow in tufts (See Manual). It is not so tall as C. stricta and the spikes are shorter and thicker. The plant is strict, usually bluish. It grows this side the pumping works.

Yours truly, L. H. Bailey, Jr.

Mr. Walter Deane,
Brewster Place,
Cambridge, Mass.

Agricultural College, Mich,
June 10, 86

My Dear Deane:

I am glad that you have found Carex panicea. It grows only about Boston. Would like enough to distribute in my set. I have found C. alopecoidea It is either rare or very generally overlooked. Yours L. H. Bailey, Jr.

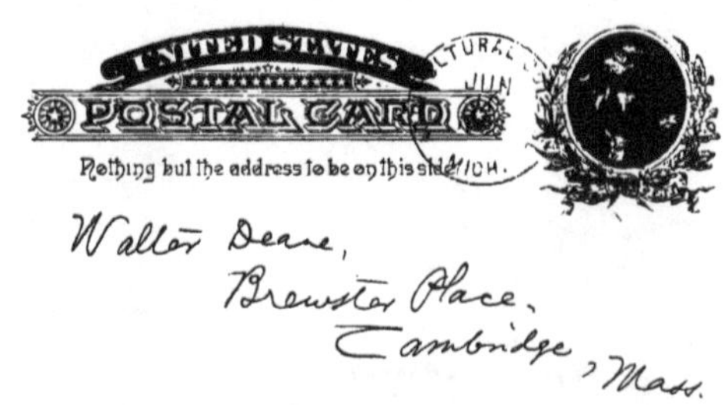

UNITED STATES
POSTAL CARD
Nothing but the address to be on this side.

Walter Deane,
Brewster Place.
Cambridge, Mass.

My Dear Deane:

The tracings are perfectly satisfactory. I am under great obligations to you for them.

C. Richardsoni from Illinois is good.

Bebb has sent me a fine lot of willows.

I have Mr. Watson's Contribution xiii.

I got out for a good long walk yesterday. Although the day was very hot, I enjoyed the cool shade and the clean luxuriant verdure of the woods. How I long for some congenial soul when I botanize! I wish that you might have been with me. Of course I looked first for Carices. I rediscovered C. arida. It is not yet ripe. In 10 days I shall visit the place again and shall hope to get enough for my set. Of course I shall remember you with one of my sets. In my student days I found C. arida far off in deep woods, but the locality is now denuded. Last year I found one poor plant. I was pleased enough to find it again. It is rare and odd. I also found C. Steudelii. Had never seen it growing before. I re-

59 of the Manual species of Carices. That is a good many for one locality. I still hope to find C. trisperma, C. flava, C. conjuncta, C. decomposita, C. squarrosa, C. aperta, C. miliacea (now C. prasina Wahl.) and C. debilis. I am losing all patience with C. gracillima. It varies abominably. I find that C. Buxbaumii varies much also. How different these Carices look in the woods and fields from those in the herbarium! The habit is often singular. That of C. arida is especially. Yesterday I visited the place where I found C. formosa a few days ago and found more of it. I also found C. Deweyana in abundance. It looks odd when growing. Oh, for no care but to botanize these bewitching June days!

L. H. Bailey, Jr.

Your no. 1 is C. vestita. No 2 is
C. canescens. I am not clear on
that Thaspium business. The specimen
you send is the same as I have always
referred to the type. Your C. panicea is
O.K. Good. Can you spare 25 spec? You
will not be too late for C. vulgaris. Took a
tramp to-day and found enough C. Hitchcock-
iana for set. Also found another new to this
locality — nothing less than the rare C.
Careyana!! 15 spec.! L. H. B. Jr. 6/14

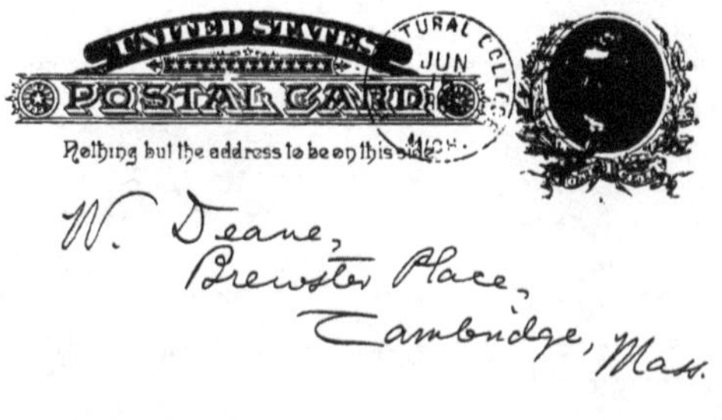
UNITED STATES
POSTAL CARD
Nothing but the address to be on this side.
JUN
MICH.
W. Deane,
Brewster Place,
Cambridge, Mass.

Your No. 3 is evidently C. filiformis, although there were not enough leaves with it to make sure that it is not the var. latifolia. Glad you found Glaux. I have only an indifferent specimen from Europe. Busy.

As ever,

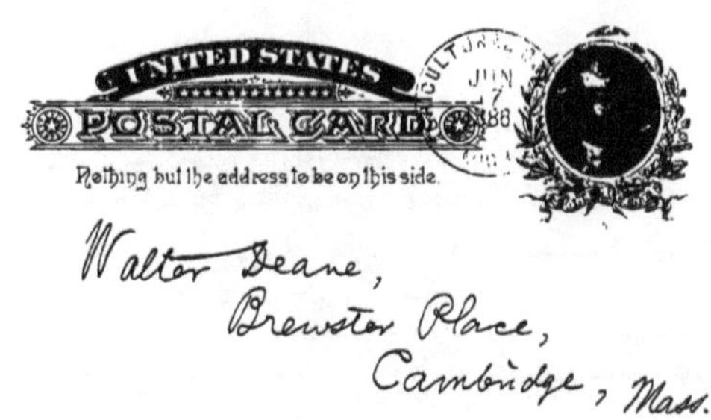

Walter Deane,
Brewster Place,
Cambridge, Mass.

DEPARTMENT OF
HORTICULTURE AND LANDSCAPE
GARDENING,

Agricultural College, Mich., June 21, 1886.

My Dear Deane:

What a boon is fellowship! I am interested in your botanizings almost as much as if they were my own. What a pitiable creature a selfish botanist must be! For instance of the contrary, when you find Hottonia, it is just the same as if I had found it: I am to have a specimen.

Carex 4 is C. muricata L.
5 & 6 are C. adusta Boott.

Would like some of each of course — of the first 15 or 20 spec. if you can get them. It is common in many places about Cambridge.

Nothing new.

L. H. Bailey, Jr.

The plants are just at hand. Have not had time to open them. Don't send labels for each spec. I will have labels printed. If you happen to be where there is any C. tentaculata get me a set. It don't grow here. I want it for comparison with C. hystricina. Don't put yourself to any trouble, however.

June 23. C. H. B. J.

Walter Deane,
Brewster Place,
Cambridge, Mass.

DEPARTMENT OF
HORTICULTURE AND LANDSCAPE
GARDENING.

Agricultural College, Mich., June 9 1886

My Dear Deane:

In two weeks I start for a camping-out expedition northwest of Lake Superior under auspices of the Minn. Geological Survey. We shall make our headquarters at Vermillion Lake, Minn., about 30 miles from the British boundary. The country is entirely [illegible]. Shall camp in the woods about three weeks. Arthur and Underwood are going and perhaps Dudley of Cornell. This will probably be one of the finest botanizing grounds in the continent. This trip may keep us away from Buffalo. Mrs. Bailey will probably go to Minneapolis and remain there with friends and relatives.

I shall begin at once to set myself at work preparing for the journey. Wish you could go.

Yours as ever,

L. H. Bailey, Jr.

[illegible] Agril College, Mich. June 30, 1886

The specimens are C. tentaculata alright.
If I could do just as I want I should like to distributo it in the condition you have coll. and also in mature state. I will make up about 15 sets and sell most of them. I will get some good things up north. I have made a list of 38 Carices which I must find there. I shall make sets for distribution of my entire collections there.

L. H. B. jr.

UNITED STATES
POSTAL CARD
Nothing but the address to be on this side.
Brewster Place
Walter Deane,
Cambridge, Mass.

Agric. Coll. July 1, '86

I am very glad that you have so many spec. of C. adusta and C. muricata for me. When I return from the N. I may be able to pay you. Mrs. Owen may have a set of Carices. Do they not want a set of my northern plants? Shall make several sets for sale.

L. H. Bailey, Jr.

UNITED STATES
POSTAL CARD
Nothing but the address to be on this side.
AGRICULTURAL
JUL 1 1886
MICH
Walter Deane,
Brewster Place,
Cambridge, Mass.

Agric. College, July 2, '86

My Dear Deane:

I have sent to Mr. Watson a package which contains a parcel of plants for you. Call for it at the Gardens. Some of the plants you may not want but you can use them in exchanges.

L. H. Bailey, Jr.

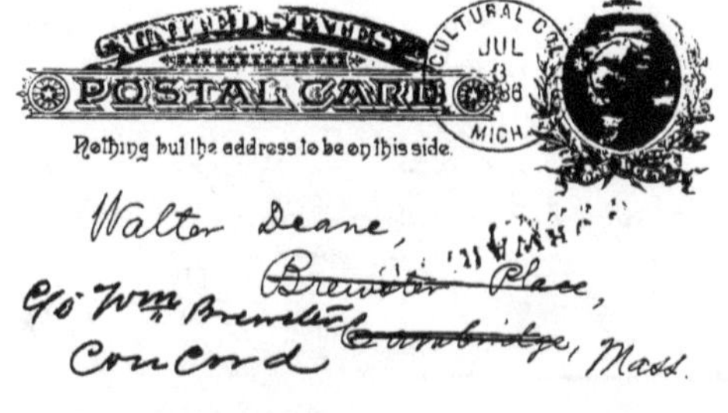
UNITED STATES
POSTAL CARD
Nothing but the address to be on this side.

CULTURAL CO
JUL
3
88
MICH

Walter Deane,
~~Brewster Place~~,
C/o Wm Brewster ~~Cambridge~~, Mass.
Concord

Michigan Agricultural College,

COLLEGE FACULTY.

[illegible]

HORTICULTURAL DEPARTMENT.

Agricultural College P. O.,
Ingham Co., Mich. June 8 1886

My Dear Deane:

The package is at hand and the contents are very nice. The C. muricata especially is fine. Your specimens will undoubtedly be the best in my set. You shall have my Minn. plants. I shall be very glad of C. bullata. The "C. vulgaris" from Chilliwack is C. stricta.

I start for the north next Tuesday or Wednesday. I go to Duluth and then take a boat along the north shore, then plunge in the "wilderness". Address me at Tower, St. Louis Co., Minnesota.

Glad that you are at Concord. Save anything of especial interest for me.

Yours ~ L. H. Bailey, Jr.

St. Paul, Minn. July 16 1886
6:30 P.M.

My Dear Deane:

I've just time for a line. Am having a nice time. Went to Minnehaha to-day. I have saved for you specimens which I picked in the spray of "Minnehaha, laughing water". I waded the stream above just where the water breaks over the precipice and secured fine fruiting specimens of Amorpha fruticosa from a bush which [illegible]d nearly over the brink. You shall have some of this also for

Minneapolis and St. Paul are beautiful cities, especially the former. I spent last night with my wife 30 miles n. w. of here. She will remain in this vicinity while I am in the woods. Go to Duluth to-night.

Y'rs Ever,

L. H. Bailey, Jr.

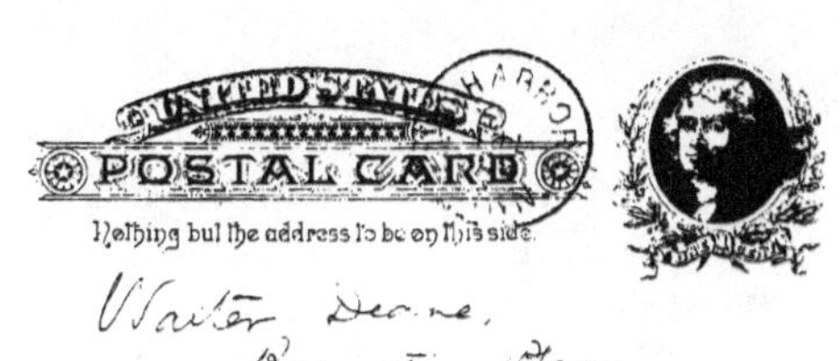

Walter Deane,
Brewster Place,
Cambridge,

College, Aug. 5, '9[illegible]

My Dear Deane: Home at last, tough and voracious. Will give you some account of my trip later. Had a good time. Yours of 25 ult. from Wells just reached me. Should like the Carex oligosperma for set. Shall not need the specimens for a month. Did you get my package yet? Regards to Mrs. D.

Yours

L. A. B. Jr.

UNITED STATES
POSTAL CARD
Nothing but the address to be on this side.
W. Deane,
Brewster Place,
Cambridge, Mass.

MICHIGAN

State Agricultural College.

Programme of Commencement Week.

1886.

SUNDAY, AUGUST 15, 3 P. M.

BACCALAUREATE ADDRESS BY PRESIDENT WILLITS.

×

WEDNESDAY, AUGUST 18, 10 A. M.

COMMENCEMENT EXERCISES.

×

WEDNESDAY, AUGUST 18, 8 TO 10 P. M.

PRESIDENT'S RECEPTION.

Shall not go to Buffalo. Am very busy.
Will write a letter soon.
L. H. B. Aug. 14.

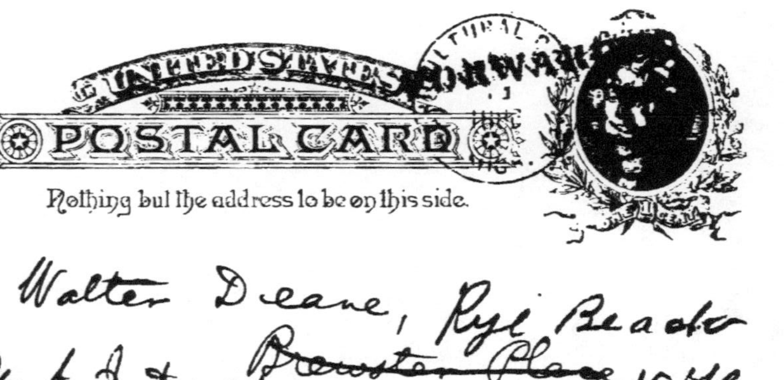

UNITED STATES

POSTAL CARD

Nothing but the address to be on this side.

Walter Deane, Rye Beach

C/o L. J. Drake, ~~Brewster Place~~ N. H.

~~Cambridge~~, ~~Mass.~~

Michigan Agricultural College,

HORTICULTURAL DEPARTMENT,

Agricultural College P. O.
Ingham Co., Mich. Aug. 15 1886.

My Dear Deane:

I have just a few minutes in which to drop you a note. I have finally given up going to Buffalo, although it was a great denial to do so. All my Minnesota collection remains to be worked up and I have all my notes of the trip to get in shape. I collected nearly 500 plants, nearly all of them in duplicate. Of three or four Carices I must have secured 100 spec. each. I also collected insects. Aside from this I travelled more than any other of the party.

Our term closes next Tuesday. We have a week's recess. That week I shall devote to botanical work. My next term will be a hard and busy one. I must get my work caught up as much as possible.

The Carex from Concord River is so fragmentary that I am not sure about it. I should guess it to be C. monile. I should much like Glaux maritima. I have Juncus Gerardi and Greenei in sufficient quantity. If you have any chance to get will do you good.

I find that it is time for me to make preparations to attend baccalaureate sermon. Let me hear from you often.

Yours sincerely,

L. H. Baily, Jr.

Michigan Agricultural College,

HORTICULTURAL DEPARTMENT.

Agricultural College P. O.,
Ingham Co., Mich. Aug. 24 1886

My Dear Deane:

Your letter of the 9th inst. was very welcome. I am glad to know ~~that~~ you are enjoying your vacation so much. I was much interested in your note on the use made of Hierochloa by the Indians.

Do you want specimens of Aster puniceus var. lucidulus? I found a patch of it to-day.

I have considerable Carex straminea v. moniliformis. With the specimens that your friends have for me I shall probably have sufficient. I have enough of the pseudo-cyperus, thanks.

I finished reading proof on my Carex matter four or five days ago. The contribution will comprise some over a

Michigan Agricultural College,

HORTICULTURAL DEPARTMENT.

Agricultural College P. O.,

Ingham Co., Mich. 188

hundred pages. I am now waiting for my 200 extras. They ought to be along in two weeks. Day after to-morrow my lectures begin again. A week's vacation is a nuisance, but I ought to be satisfied for this summer.

Do you want Aster junceus and Solidago stricta?

Must close. Let me hear from you often. Regards to Mrs. D.

Yours as ever,

L. H. Bailey, Jr.

My Dear Deane: Sept. 2. 80 M.

By this time I suppose you are home again thinking about a winter of teaching. I will lay aside the plants for you. I have not yet undone all my Minnesota plants. I can't get time to get at them. I lecture every day to 52 bright young men.

Yours Truly, L. H. Bailey, Jr.

UNITED STATES
POSTAL CARD
Nothing but the address to be on this side
MICH.
Mr. Walter Deane,
Brewster Place,
Cambridge,

Michigan Agricultural College,

HORTICULTURAL DEPARTMENT.

Agricultural College P. O.:
Ingham Co., Mich. Sept. 8 188 5.

My Dear Deane:

The package of plants is at hand in good condition, The plants are very nice. Please accept thanks, very many. I shall be glad to incorporate them in my set.

Churchill's sedge, although more erect than yours, is C. straminea v. moniliformis

The plant which you returned for a label is Chenopodium (Blitum) Bonus-Henricus.

I shall be glad to look over the carices for your friend, and especially so as they were collected by Thoreau whom I much admire. I almost covet the specimens.

Yes, I should like a Woodwardia when

you are sending again. Shall be glad of the fruit of Plantago decipiens, also. Remember us both to Mrs. Deane.

Again with thanks, Deane,

Yours as ever,

L. H. Bailey, Jr.

Michigan Agricultural College,

HORTICULTURAL DEPARTMENT.

Agricultural College P. O.
Ingham Co., Mich. Sept. 20 1886.

My Dear Deane:

I have not heard from you in some time. I suppose that you are busy getting started off in your school again. All last week I was at the State Fair at Jackson, and as I had charge of a large part of the horticultural exhibit I had no time to write.

Things are going on as usual. Cold and windy to-day. "The melancholy days are come".

My work is awaiting me.

Let me hear from you.

Yours as ever,

L. H. Bailey, Jr.

Aug. 25.

The fine perigynia are at hand. I am under great obligations for them. I wrote you that I did not want any but I did not then think of sending a pocket with each specimen. You are very kind to think of me.

Yours as ever,

L. H. B. Jr.

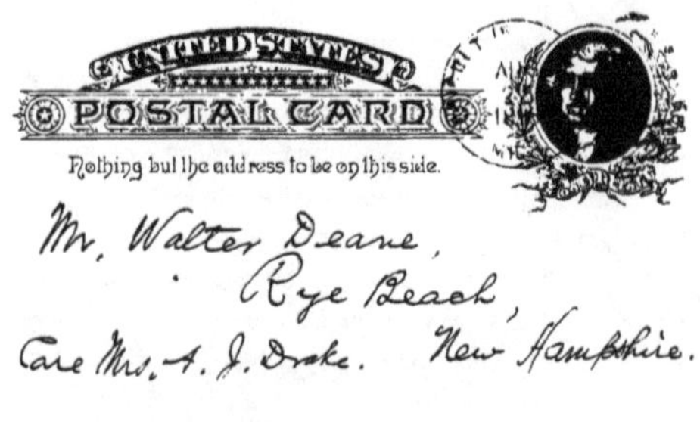
UNITED STATES
POSTAL CARD
Nothing but the address to be on this side.

Mr. Walter Deane,
Rye Beach,
Care Mrs. A. J. Drake. New Hampshire.

Michigan Agricultural College,

HORTICULTURAL DEPARTMENT.

Agricultural College P. O.
Ingham Co., Mich. Sept. 26 1886

My Dear Deane:

Yours of the 22nd inst. is just at hand. I find ~~that I~~ have both Ruppia and Zannichellia from near Boston, collected by myself. I evidently gave you the wrong plant. I have a large specimen of Centaurea nigra which I collected in 1883 beyond Arlington.

I do not progress at all with my sets. I must make an inventory of my department, write my annual report and complete a bulletin next week. When that is all done I shall go at my plants. Have not named my Minnesota collections yet. Hope to have my sets ready by the middle of Oct. Will look for my Carex synopses next week. Beside all my other work for next week, including teaching + looking after students' labor, I take part in the

Michigan Agricultural College,

COLLEGE FACULTY.

Edwin Willits, M. A.,	President.	
T. C. Abbot, LL. D.,	Prof. of	Mental Science.
R. C. Kedzie, M. A., M. D.,	"	Chemistry.
A. J. Cook, M. A.,	"	Entomology.
W. J. Beal, M. S., Ph. D.,	"	Botany.
R. C. Carpenter, M. S., C. E.,	"	Mathematics.
Sam'l Johnson,	"	Agriculture.
E. J. MacEwan, M. A.,	"	English.
E. A. A. Grange, V. S.,	"	Veterinary.
J. A. Lockwood, Lt. U. S. A.,	"	Military Science.
L. H. Bailey, Jr., B. S.,	"	Horticulture.
Lewis McLouth, M. A., Ph. D.,	"	Mechanics.

HORTICULTURAL DEPARTMENT.

Agricultural College P. O.

Ingham Co., Mich. ......188..

Central Michigan Fair to be held at Lansing.

I had intended to make a flying trip to Cambridge this winter, to lecture again before the State Agricultural Soc. but I find that I cannot have time to prepare a lecture, so I have given up the trip.

I hear that Mr. Watson is in Europe.

If you go again to the sea-coast don't forget the pits of Prunus maritima.

Regards of us both to Mrs. G.

Yours &c

L. H. Bailey, Jr.

Overdone Camp,
Hoodoo Point,
Onamanni-sagieagan,
48th parallel,
July 18, 1886.

My Dear Deane:

Here we are at 9 P.M. in our tent writing and studying by the light of a candle on the lonely shores of Onamanni-sagieagan (as near as I can write the Indian pronunciation), or Vermilion Lake. The wind blows furiously and whirls snap our tent and thunder and the roar of waves keep it company. At times it rains furiously. Still we try to be happy, three of us, Arthur, Holway, and myself. My bed of Abies balsamea and Thuja is fragrant and invites me to sleep as soon as I have said something to my friend far off in the East.

N. of Lake Superior. The wild winds bring us no tidings

from civilization. Indians are everywhere. Pashetonequeo is our cook. He is a short and good natured Indian who to-day brought Mrs. Pashetone-qweb and little Pashetonequeb to spend Sunday with him. They lie on the ground, bare headed, in rain or shine and appear to be happy. Mrs. Pashetonegweb does not speak English. None of the Indians speak much. They are Chippewas. I am trying to get their names of plants. Waupekoon is Epilobium spicatum. Otay-emin (pl. Otayeminin) is the strawberry.

The first Carex I found is C. Houghtonii. The second is possibly a new species. The third is C. pratensis, new to the U.S.

Think of your friend away off in the interminable wilderness.

Yours ... [illegible]

Address me at
Tower, St. Louis Co.,
Minnesota

My Dear Deane:

No, I have not Cyperus Engelmanni. Would like a specimen very much.

I congratulate you upon the amount of work you have been able to do in your herbarium. It is delightful work, but I get almost no time to do it.

Was sorry to hear of Mr. Churchill's illness. As you said nothing about it in your last letter, I trust that he is getting better. There is considerable typhoid in Lansing.

Shall be glad of Aster tenuifolius.

I don't know how you will succeed with Wheeler. Formerly he was one of the most delightful of correspondents but of late business has so engrossed his attention that I can't get much out of him. Write him, anyway. Tell him that I referred you to him.

I was glad of the little Gratiola. I found it in that form once in Mystic Pond.

I have written an "ad" for Gazette saying that I had a few sets of Carices for $3.50 each.

The grass you return is evidently E. tenella.

It is late and I am tired.

Yours as ever,

L. H. Bailey, Jr.

Agricultural College, Mich.,
Oct. 7, '86.

My Dear Deane: I have before me two of your letters, unanswered. The pkts of Chinese writing were very acceptable. Your name will be printed in our next report among the donors. I am now getting a little time to put on my northern collection. I have mounted nearly half of them. I secured very few rare things. Before the term closes I want to mount my loose carices of the summer's getting — some 200 or 300 sheets. I am afraid, however, that I can't get to it. Term closes four weeks from last Friday. As soon as it closes, we shall go to my father's for a two weeks' visit, then to Grand

12,000 people.
Regards from us both to yourself and Mrs. D.
Yours as ever,
L. H. Bailey Jr.

Rapids to attend the winter meeting of the State Horticultural Society, and then back to Lansing for the winter. I shall put most of my time this winter on German, and Mrs. Bailey will put hers on French. I will have no cares to work up this winter. Dr Gray writes that he has rec'd my "[illegible] Carex Synopsis," so I suppose it is out and I will get my extras in a week or so. It has "hung fire" a long time.

I should like to see Sukedorf.

We have had a magnificent autumn, but rain and storm are breaking it up now. Now comes good weather for indoor work. I enjoyed your account to Concord River. I never yet got fruit of any of the Nymphaeas.

I shall appreciate very much the photograph of Fiscian.

A few days ago I gave a lecture on "Origination of Cultural Varieties" before a Hort. Society at Eaton Rapids in this state, and I am invited to give another lecture there next month.

The legislature convenes this winter and Lansing will be aglow with life. The little city is growing very rapidly. A number of miles of street car track were constructed this summer and a new and extensive system of water works was put in. The city is small but thriving — some 10,000 to

My Dear Deane:

My Carex Synopses have come at last. I send you one.

It will do you good to look up the Texan plants and you will get a good lot of plants too.

I was much pleased with Thoreau's picture. Many thanks.

I am about half through with my Minn. plants. Patterson cannot get my labels done for a couple weeks yet, so cannot get my Carices off this month.

Yours as ever,

L. H. Bailey, Jr.

Thanks for the pockets of fruits. I like to have the fruit separate in ~~that~~ way.

My Dear Deane: I sent a Carex
Synopsis to Mr. Kennedy, addressing
it to him at "The Pines, Milton, Mass."
It now occurs to me that I
should have sent it to Readville. If
so, please notify him to have it
forwarded. Yours &c.

Oct. 28.

L. H. Bailey, Jr.

Walter Deane,
Cambridge,
Brewster Place. Mass.

My Dear Dunne:

Your list of synonyms is correct, unless it be in the case of that puzzling old Carex mirabilis. The Carex cristata var. mirabilis intended by manual is not C. tribuloides var. cristata in part, for it is not quite the same thing as C. mirabilis Dewey. All the manual vars. of C. straminea are Boott's. The var. tenera of the Manual is C. straminea. The plant which I designated in Bot. Gaz. x. 381 as var. tenera Boott is var. aperta. The mix occurs thus: Dewey made Carex tenera. Boott reduced what he supposed to be Dewey's C. tenera to var. tenera, but Boott did not describe the plant that

So, you see, Booth's Var. tenera is one thing and the Var. tenera I described is another. Now it so happens that Booth had described as Var. aperta the true C. tenera of Dewey. Now Sartwell, Carey &c., described as C. tenera the same plant which Booth had made Var. tenera; hence my references on p. 149 of Synopsis "C. tenera, Sartwell . . . not Dewey," "C. straminea var. tenera Boott". And on p. 152, under Var. aperta, I cite the original true C. tenera of Dewey, and my var. tenera. See?

to the three that I never could get before: C. limosa & stygia, the exceedingly rare C. deciduas and C. podocarpa.

Glad you like my Synopsis. Am receiving many congratulatory letters.

Is Churchill's address Dorchester? Will be glad to send him a copy.

Where shall I send Mrs. Owen's. Does she want a set of my Carices?

Your corrections are at hand.

I have never got C. echinata from this country. I may have European specimens for you. Will look.

My lecture is not in print yet.

Have heard from Kennedy. He rec'd Synopsis.

This is almost unreadable, but I am

My Dear Deane:

You ask what I won't do next. I shall not vote for Blaine if he secures presidential nomination.

To-morrow I shall send to Dr. Gray a bundle of plants. Some of them are for you. Call at the Gardens for them. You will find a few of my northern plants which are unnamed. Will you compare them and report by numbers?

Term closes to-morrow. Saturday we shall move into Lansing. We had intended to go for two weeks to South Haven, but Mrs. B. is not feeling able to go at present. Fine weather for November.

Yours in a hurry,

L. H. Bailey, Jr.

SUPPLEMENT

To the Catalogue of North American Carices.

While it is not intended to keep the Catalogue of North American Carices abreast with the latest nomenclature, it is nevertheless thought proper that the following additions and corrections, being of importance, should be inserted:

ADDITIONS.

CAREX
affinis, R. Br.: see obtusata.
Assiniboinensis, W. Boott. n. sp. *Br. Am.*
brizoides, L.
  var. nemoralis, Wimm. *Arc. Am.*
Ehrenbergiana, Bœckler. *Mex.*
Fendleriana, Bœckler. *New Mex.*
glauca, Scop. *Canada.* *(Introd.)*
heptastachya, Bœckler. *Costa Rica.*
interrupta, Bœckler. *Oregon.*
  (C. verticillata, Boott. C. angustata, var. verticillata, Boott.)
Jamesii, Torr.
  var. Nebraskensis. *W. States.*
  (C. Nebraskensis, Dewey.)
Magellanica, Lam. *N. S. and N., Ry. Mts.*
  (C. irrigua, Smith.)
pauciflora, Lightf. *N. S. and N., Ry. Mts.*
ptychocarpa, Steud. *La.*
Saskatschawana, Bœckler. *Br. Am.*
spiculosa, Fries? *Near Boston.*
straminea, Schk.
  var. invisa, W. Boott, n. var. *Me. to Mass.*
truncata, Bœckler. *La.*

EMENDATIONS.

For C. angustata, Boott, var. verticillata, Boott, read:
angustata, Boott, var. verticillata, Boott: see interrupta.
For C. canescens, L., var. vitilis, Carey, read:
canescens, L.
  var. alpicola, Wahl. *E. S. and N.*
  (var. vitilis, Carey.)
For C. Fraseriana, Sims, read:
Fraseri, Andrews.
For C. Grahamii, Boott, read:
Grahamii, Boott: see saxatilis.
Cancel C. invisa, W. Boott. *(See straminea.)*
For C. irrigua, Smith, read:
irrigua, Smith: see Magellanica.
After C. Lemmoni, insert n. sp., and cancel *Ariz.*
For C. Lyallii, Boott, read:
Lyallii, Boott: see Raynoldsii.
After C. monile, Tuckm., insert:
  (Including C. Vaseyi, Dewey.)
Refer C. monosperma, Macoun, to gynocrates.
For C. Vaseyi, Dewey, read:
Vaseyi, Dewey: see monile.

Whole number of species catalogued, 200; varieties, 85.

L. H. BAILEY, Jr.

Cambridge, May 1, 1884.

My Dear Deane:

I was out to the College to-day and found the plants awaiting me. They are very nice. Accept thanks. The Carices under No. 31 are Carex canescens L. v. alpicola Wahl., C. echinata Murr., v. microstachys Boeckl., and var. conferta Bailey, C. scoparia Schkuhr. I did not have time to make a critical examination of No. 30. It looks like Carex vulgaris. It may be the same as Churchill's which I called C. stricta. The two species are very similar and are to be distinguished by habit more than by anything else. I will look up Churchill's plants again and make a critical examination.

The C. cristata var. mirabilis of the Manual is mixed. It is mainly straminea v. mirabilis, but the rest of it goes probably mostly to tribuloides v. cristata. Your 3 sheets from Willoughby are C. tribuloides v. cristata. I now understand ~~that~~ variety. They are named as in the Synopsis.

Was glad to have Robb's opinion. As it was given without my knowledge, I suppose that I may take it at par.

be at Grand Rapids.

For the winter address me at

Mrs. Bailey is feeling pretty well

wishes to be remembered.

Again thanks for the very interesting

Yours truly,

L. H. Bailey

Persons receiving this programme are requested to forward short notes of experience and opinions upon any of the topics to be read and published in connection with the proceedings of the convention.

Information concerning the meeting will be gladly furnished on application, and all communications should be addressed to

CHAS. W. GARFIELD, Secretary,

Grand Rapids, Michigan.

MICHIGAN
State Horticultural Society

OF THE

ANNUAL MEETING

TO BE HELD IN

GRAND RAPIDS, MICH.,

Tuesday, Wednesday & Thursday,
Nov. 30th, and Dec. 1st and 2d.
1886

FULL LIST OF ANNOUNCEMENTS AND SCHEME OF TOPICS.

Reduced Fare on all Railroads and Minimum Hotel Rates.

A GREAT MEETING.

STATE

Horticultural Society.

PROGRAMME

For the Annual Meeting of 1886, to convene in Grand Rapids Nov. 30th and Dec. 1st and 2d.

ANNOUNCEMENT.

The [illegible] Annual meeting of the Michigan Horticultural Society, will convene in Grand Rapids, in acceptance of an invitation from the Grand River Valley Horticultural Society. It was here that the Society was organized, in 1870, and the convention which has now been planned, promises to be one of unusual interest and importance. Upon the understanding that there will be [illegible] visiting delegates, the railroads have granted excursion rates, and all who are to attend should send to the Secretary for certificates, AT ONCE.

[illegible] at the rate of ONE DOLLAR per day. The offer was accepted and the Eagle Hotel will be headquarters for the Society. [illegible]

The convention will open with an evening session on November 30, and close with the lecture on the evening of December 2d.

[illegible]

[illegible]

The general public are invited to attend the meetings and participate in the discussions. The following is an outline of the proceedings which may be varied in the arrangement of topics for the day meetings.

SCHEME OF TOPICS.

TUESDAY EVENING.

7:30 o'clock. 1—Reading of Correspondence.
2—President's Annual Address.
3—Reports of Officers.
4—Report of Committee on Legislation.
5—[illegible]
6—Appointment of Committees for the convention.

WEDNESDAY MORNING SESSION.

9 o'clock. 1—Election of Officers for ensuing year.
2—Are Michigan Apples deteriorating?
3—[illegible]
4—[illegible] old Apple Orchards.
5—Upon what does Future Successful Apple-growing Depend?
6—[illegible]

AFTERNOON SESSION.

[illegible]

[illegible]

EVENING SESSION.

7 o'clock. [illegible]
8 o'clock. Address by Hon. Edwin Willits, President of the State Agricultural College; Subject: [illegible]

THURSDAY MORNING SESSION.

9 o'clock. [illegible]
12:30 o'clock. Address by [illegible]

AFTERNOON SESSION.

1:30 o'clock. Reports of Standing Committees of the Society.
2:30 o'clock. The Public Park a [illegible]
1—[illegible] of Cities and Villages.
2—A Place of Legitimate Recreation.
3—An Educator.
4—[illegible]
5—[illegible]
6—[illegible]

EVENING SESSION.

7 o'clock. Reports of Committees.
8 o'clock. Lecture by Prof. [illegible] of Amherst, Massachusetts; Subject: [illegible]
Final Resolutions—Adjournment.

n Mr G...ca..
d that you like
plants. I re-
n to Lansing in
morning Tuesda
o to Grand Rap
e no Minn. plan
ode, I sent abo
the desirable
...v of ...ing
ie duplicates,
nks for the verifi
ons. Yes!—

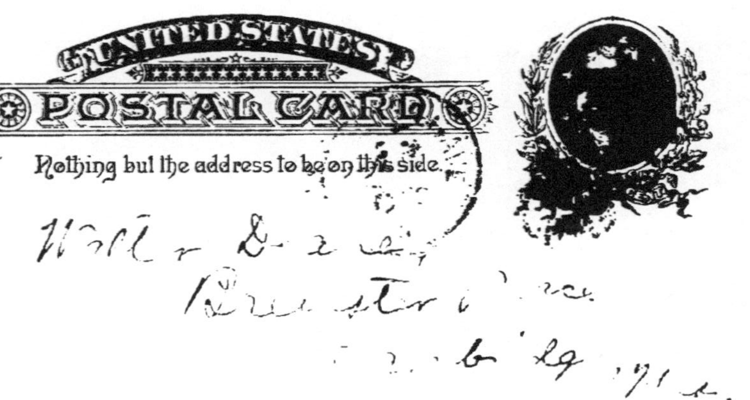
UNITED STATES
POSTAL CARD
Nothing but the address to be on this side.

My Dear Deane: Upon arriving home from Grand Rapids I find your letter of the 28th ult. Thanks for the determination. I was at the College to-day but did not have time to look up your questions. I did look at that sheet of Carices, no. 51, and find four as you say: C. scoparia, C. echinata v. conferta & v. microstachys and the canescens var.

Carex alpina is rare evidently and I have no duplicates unless one or two from Europe.

I find that I have lost Mrs. [illegible] address.

Mr. Anthony, who lived down stairs at 860 Main St, died a few days ago with typhoid fever. His wife is sick with the same, we hear.

We are pretty well. Mrs. B. will be [illegible] Cold.

Had a very pleasant letter from A. W. Chapman a few days ago.

Mich.

Vacation closes Feb. 22.

I am surprised that my smooth [illegible] Pent-stemon is P. pubescens.

Sometime when you are at the gardens please look in Booth's Index, vol. IV, and in Kunth and see if there is a Carex pinguis. Look also in Boeckeler's Indexes (Linnaea, vols. [illegible], 40 & 41.

Regards to Mrs. D.

Yours truly,

L. H. Bailey

INGHAM COUNTY

Horticultural Society.

PROGRAMME

For First Half of 1887.

SATURDAY, Jan. 8th—Discussion on Cold Storage for Fruits. Led by GEO. W. PARK and WILSON MOORE.

SATURDAY, Feb. 12th—Methods and Results of Budding and Grafting. Discussion led by object lessons, by C. S. CRANDALL, Agricultural College.

SATURDAY, March 12th—Adornment of Yards and Streets. Led by DR. W. J. BEAL, Agricultural College.

SATURDAY, April 9th—General Discussion on the Plans of the Season, with especial reference to Methods of Culture of Vegetables and Small Fruits.

SATURDAY, May 14th—Plant Diseases. Led by DR. MANLY MILES, Lansing.

SATURDAY, June 11—Annual Spring Flower Exhibit. Date liable to change to conform to the season. Premiums will be offered.

These meetings are entirely informal and everyone is invited to attend and to take part in the discussions. The meetings are held in the Pioneer Rooms, in the Capitol, (reached by elevator from basement) at 2 o'clock, standard time.

The place of meeting is liable to be changed, but notice of change will be given through the press.

L. H. BAILEY, Jr.,
President.

C. B. STEBBINS,
Secretary.

THORP & GODFREY PRINTERS, LANSING.

My Dear Deane:

Merry Christmas!

I have looked over the carices from Lloyd, and will return them soon. The no. 6 from Mrs. Owen is a puzzle. As you say, the staminate flowers are at the top, but that does not make it C. muricata by a long way. The first specimen I had was so much shattered that I could find no staminate flowers. I never saw a Carex like it before. There is a possibility of its being some odd European variety of C. muricata, but I doubt it. Compare the perigynia of this with that of C. muricata. They are widely dissimilar. Can you get any more spec. of it? Would like to know just where and under what circumstances it grew.

Dewey died in 1872 Don't know about

Carex. See the bibliography in my last Carex paper. That will give you an idea.

Yours truly,

L. H. Bailey, Jr.

My Dear Deane:

Some time since I purchased John Burrough's Wake Robin. I was so pleased with it that I resolved to buy Pepacton. What was my surprise and delight to receive that volume from you! You could not have made a better selection. I am under obligations for the remembrance. The snow is eight inches deep and sleighing is excellent. We take a twist about the city every day.

Remember us both to Mrs. D.

Happy New Year!

Yours truly,

L. H. Bailey, Jr.

I have a question to ask: In the manual the paper birch is Betula papyracea of Aiton. The name is now written B. papyrifera. Do you know who is authority for it? I think Marshall.

Donnelly House,
M. J. Donnelly, Prop.

Good Sample Rooms for Agents.

Mason, Mich Dec. 30 1886

My Dear Deane:

Yours of the 27th is in my hands.

I am glad to know about the Triglochin. Will look up the Fraxinus.

Yes, I noticed the mistake, C. longirostrata, in index. There are three or four typographical errors in the paper.

I am here to give a lecture this evening. I am getting tired of this lecture business and am tempted to give it up.

Snow 15 in. deep and sleighing

HUDSON HOUSE.
M. HUDSON, PROPRIETOR.

Lansing, Mich. Jan. 6 1887

My Dear Deane:
My Carex article in Dec. Gazette will explain that C. arctata x flexilis matter. I had supposed that that article would appear before I sent out my set. It has been in the hands of the editors since September.
Mark what carices you have on the enclosed list and return. If I get others, I will remember you.
Thanks for information in regard to Betula papyrifera.
Lots of snow and superb sleighing.
Yours ever,
L. H. Bailey, Jr

Lansing, Jan. 6. '87.

I went up to the College this morning and did up your Carices and sent them. I did not send the one from Churchill for I want to look at it again. As soon as I get time to make a critical examination I can probably determine it. Yes, "gracillima" in Gazette is printer's error for "debilis". Your Hierochloa article is good. L. H. B. Jr.

UNITED STATES
POSTAL CARD
Nothing but the address to be on this side.
Walter Deane,
Brewster Place,
Cambridge, Mass.

Lansing, Mich., Jan. 8, '87

My Dear Deane:

Yesterday I went to the College and had time to make a critical examination of that Nantucket Carex, and found that it is simply an unusual form of Carex Muhlenbergii! How these sedges do perplex one! I often think that I know nothing about them.

As soon as I get time I shall make a critical examination of that C. vulgaris of yours.

We are having a model winter. For over a month we have had clear weather and superb sleighing, and although it is sometimes a little chilly (28° below zero night before last), it is not enough so to be uncomfortable.

I spend a good deal of time at the Legislature. I don't know that I ever told you that I have a bill for some $8000 before that body for the equipment of my department. Consequently I must see that it passes. I propose to have a building for my work, and apparatus to do with.

Wife and I had a fine ride last night in the clear moonlight although the mercury hid itself away below zero.

Yours truly,
L. H. Bailey, Jr.

Lansing, Jan. 26.

My Dear D.—

I am going to move back to the college in 10 days. I will leave your Carices till then. I am very busy now. Glad to hear that you visited Kennedy

Yours—

L. H. B. Jr.

UNITED STATES

POSTAL CARD

Nothing but the address to be on this side.

Walter Deane,
Brewster Place,
Cambridge, Mass.

JACKSON, MICHIGAN, Feb. 5 1887

My Dear Deane:

I have not heard from you in a long time, neither have I written. I have been very busy. Last Saturday we moved back to College, so that you must address me there hereafter. Yesterday morning I went to Hanover to attend an Institute, and now (9 P.M.) I am on my way home, spending the night in this thriving city of 20,000 people. As you will see, by the enclosed program, the people at Hanover were bored last evening.

Next week I attend another, and week after next another. I go a good deal on this business.

School opens Feb. 22. I shall be glad to get into the ruts again.

Let me hear from you.

Yours &c

L. H. Bailey, Jr.

MICHIGAN
State Horticultural Society.

Annual Membership, $1.00. Life Membership, $10.00.

Feb 9 1887.

No. 1. Carex straminea between vars
alata & foenea Nearest alata and
may pass for that.
No. 2. Good, straight C. vulgaris.
No. 3. After a very careful examination I am inclined to refer this
to C. vulgaris. It is the same as the
lot which you sent me from
Churchill last summer and
which I called C. stricta. It is
very near C. stricta at any rate.
Live plants of C. vulgaris should
have a bluish cast.
No. 4. I think a very slender form
of C. tribuloides v. reducta.
No. 5. C. scabrata

No. 6. C. vulgaris.
No. 7. C. canescens v. alpicola almost. The perigynia are the sharpest I ever saw, but it is not C. echinata. Compare with C. echinata and observe different habit, arrangement of spikes, etc.
No. 8. C. Muhlenbergii near v. enervis
No. 9. Probably C. straminea v. foenea, but can't say surely from this specm.

College, Feb. 9, '87

My Dear Deane: Arriving at home I find your two welcome letters awaiting me. We were sorry to hear of Mrs. D's illness, and hope that she is fully recovered by this time.

I congratulate you upon securing a microscope. You could not invest money better. Yes, Mrs. Owen's money came to hand in due time.

To-day I looked over your Carices, & I enclose the names. I send the plants by same mail.

Can't stop longer now.

Yours truly &c

L. H. B. Jr.

Ag. College, Feb. 22, 1887

My Dear Deane:

I was glad to get your letter with the determinations of Werner's plants.

I have a question to ask you concerning two or three French words. The word rustiques, rusticité, must mean hardy, hardiness, in technical literature, although I can find no authority for such use in the lexicons at my command. Here is a sentence to illustrate: "En effet ceux-ci, qui ont eu pour mère les Rosiers dits Indiens, qui sont remontants, mais sujets à geler, et, pour père, les Rosiers Provins, qui sont rustiques, mais qui ne remontent pas."

What is the meaning of the term <u>bourgeonnement</u>?

I go to Hillsdale this morning to attend State Hort. Convention. School opens to-day.

Yours &c
L. H. Bailey, Jr.

Michigan State Horticultural Society.

Winter Meeting of 1887 will Convene at the Court House in Hillsdale, Tuesday, Wednesday and Thursday, February 22, 23 and 24.

All persons who are interested in any branch of Horticulture and Forestry are cordially invited to attend and take part in the discussions of the convention. Those who can not attend are earnestly solicited to jot down their views briefly upon any of the topics, and send in to be read during the discussions.

Samples of fruits plants, flowers, branches, insects, implements and contrivances, if brought in, will receive attention at the hands of the Society.

Hillsdale county ranks among the best counties in the State in Agricultural and Horticultural progress, and this meeting is in acceptance of a joint invitation from the county Agricultural and Horticultural Societies.

All kindred societies, in and out of the State, are invited to send delegates. Reports from branch Horticultural Societies, and the Question Box will be features of the convention.

Scheme of Topics.

TUESDAY.

2 o'clock P. M. 1—Reasons for the Decline of Orcharding in Southern Michigan. Led by B. Hathaway, Cass County.

2 History of Horticultural Progress in Michigan, as affected by the State Society and its branches. President Lyon.

3—Suggestions for Local Societies. Secretary Garfield.

4 What can Legislation do for Horticulture in Michigan? L. D. Watkins, Manchester.

7 o'clock P. M. 1—Experience meeting for a half hour.

2 Methods and Results of Grafting, illustrated by stereoptican views Chas. S. Crandall, Lansing.

3 Commercial Fertilizers: Their Value and Uses. W. L. Snyder, Detroit.

4—Appointment of Committees.

WEDNESDAY.

9 o'clock A. M. 1—Best Way to Purchase Nursery Stock. E. H. Scott, Ann Arbor.

2—An Hour with Varieties of Apples for Culture in Southern Michigan. J. F. Fitzsimmons, Hillsdale.

3—The Development and Promises of the Evaporated Fruit Industry. S. B. Mann, Adrian, and H. W. Davis, Lapeer.

4 An Hour with the Worst Insect Pests and a Study of Remedies. R. J. Coryell, Hillsdale.

2 o'clock P. M. 1 Fall Exhibits of Fruits: Their Management and Educational Advantages, A. G. Gulley, South Haven.

2—Suggestions Concerning City and Village Horticulture. Prof. L. H. Bailey, Lansing.

3—Economic Market Culture of Potatoes: The Best Varieties. C. A. Sessions, Oceana County.

4—A Discussion Upon Potato Deterioration and Experience with the Scab.

7 o'clock P. M. 1—The Forestry Problem. F. M. Holloway, Hillsdale.

2—What Can Schools do for Horticulture, and vice versa. Prof. W. A. Drake, Hillsdale College.

3—Ethics of Horticulture. Prof. A. S. Haynes, Hillsdale, and W. K. Gibson, Jackson.

THURSDAY.

9 o'clock A. M. 1—Reports of Committees.

2—The Question Box.

3—Discussion on Markets and Marketing.

4—Final Resolutions.

It is expected that Prof's Cook and Beal, of the Agricultural College will be present and address the Society upon Destructive Insects, Forest Growing and Preservation.

Delegates are advised to get round trip tickets as far as practicable and thus save a percentage of the regular price.

All questions or communications concerning the meeting, should be addressed to

CHAS. W. GARFIELD, Secretary

GRAND RAPIDS. MICH.

DEPARTMENT OF
HORTICULTURE AND LANDSCAPE
GARDENING,

Agricultural College, Mich., Mar. 4 1887

My Dear Deane:

I have been very negligent of late. I am very hard at work. After this week I will have it a little easier.

I am very much obliged for the French. It is just what I wanted.

I supposed my Bromus to be B. sterilis because there was no other to match it in the Manual. I am glad to know that it is not. I never picked it there. I simply saw it growing. I enclose you a bit which I picked in Boston. Is it B. tectorum?

I cannot satisfy myself ~~that~~ my Fraxinus 117 is F. viridis. I have but one spec. of F. viridis and that does not match my 117, and it was named at Cambridge. 117 exactly matches speci-mens which I have al-ways taken for F. Americana. I may be mistaken however.

I have had all my Carex papers bound, the synopsis being interleaved. It makes a handy volume.

I give a lecture every day on the science of horticulture. It makes me work.

Write often.

Yours truly
L. H. Bailey, Jr.

Michigan Agricultural College,

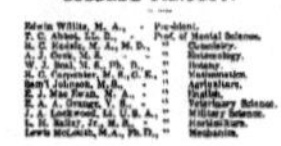

DEPARTMENT OF HORTICULTURE AND LANDSCAPE GARDENING.

Agricultural College P. O.,

Ingham Co., Mich. Mar. 24 1887

My Dear Deane:

Thanks for the note, and descriptions of the Bromuses.

I suppose that all my Fraxinus 117 came from the same tree but I cannot remember at this date.

I have been getting a few Carices of late, but scarcely any duplicates of interest. I received an interesting little bundle from Arkansas a few days ago. I have all of Mertindale's Carices here to name. Big lot and a big job. I have little time for it now. I am about half way through with them. Among them, I find one from Phila. which is new to America, — C. distans L. It should be 152a in my Synopsis. This is the first species to be added to my list. I will send you a speci-

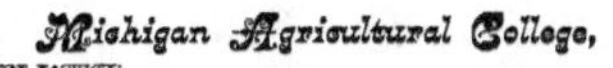

Michigan Agricultural College,

DEPARTMENT OF HORTICULTURE AND LANDSCAPE GARDENING.

Agricultural College. P. O.,

Ingham Co., Mich. .... 188....

men some day. I have made two or three new vars. since the publication of my Synopsis.

How long is Dr Gray to remain in Europe? Does he go to study, and where?

We are having an unusual March — almost like May. Catkins will be out on the poplars in a few days.

Yours ever,

L. H. Bailey, Jr.

Michigan Agricultural College,

COLLEGE FACULTY:

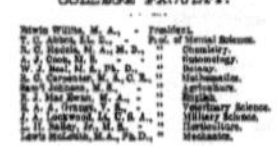

DEPARTMENT OF HORTICULTURE AND LANDSCAPE GARDENING.

Agricultural College, P. O.

Ingham Co., Mich. Ap. 8 188[illegible]

My Dear Deane:

By this time I suppose that you are at home again. We were much disappointed ~~that~~ you should almost pass our door and not look in upon us. We shall not forgive you if you ever do it again.

Our spring has received a sudden check. I will collect all I can of the plants you want. Hepaticas are out.

I have an extra specimen of the new grass — new genus — Bealia Mexicana, and I will send it to you when I send anything again.

Regards from us both to yourself and Mrs. D.

Yours &c
L. H. Bailey, Jr.

Michigan Agricultural College,

DEPARTMENT OF HORTICULTURE AND LANDSCAPE GARDENING.

Agricultural College P. O.,
Ingham Co., Mich., Apr. 29 1887

My Dear Deane:

I am glad that you both had such an enjoyable time in Chicago. In many respects it is a wonderful city.

Your note concerning Tussilago reminded me that last summer I was much surprised to find leaves of it about four miles from here. So to-day I drove there and found it in full bloom! Had never seen it in flower before. Much obliged for the reminder.

Ever since I began studying Carex I have been trying to get Olney's picture and I have finally succeeded. Now I want Carey's. I have Dewey's.

Spring comes on tediously.

Yours,
L. H. Bailey, Jr.

Michigan Agricultural College,

COLLEGE FACULTY:

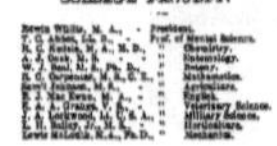

DEPARTMENT OF HORTICULTURE AND LANDSCAPE GARDENING.

Agricultural College P. O.,
Ingham Co., Mich., May 8 1887

My Dear Deane:

We have just had a warm shower and the air is laden with the perfume and freshness of balmy spring. How I long to be forever out of doors, to be forever in the embrace of this vernal charm! The fruit-trees are becoming white, the lawns and meadows are sprinkled with varied constellations and the birds are happy. In the woods almost back of my door three or four violets, the large trillium, "adder's-tongue" as we call the erythronium, the large uvularia, june-berries and flowering dogwood, hepaticas, phloxes, isopyrum, crowfoots, caltha, a half dozen sedges, and many others invite me thither. But I shall not botanize much this year. A multitude of other duties will keep me from the woods and

COLLEGE FACULTY:

DEPARTMENT OF HORTICULTURE AND LANDSCAPE GARDENING.

Agricultural College P. O.

Ingham Co., Mich. ....188....

fields. I must learn more of books. I have just rec'd from England a box containing Gerard's Herball, Tragus' Stirpium, Parkinson's Paradisus, Watson's Cybele (8 vols. $30.00), Nyman's Conspectus, etc.; also Schkuhr's Carices in French, with th plates, portrait, and all. This month I shall have Boott's grand work. I have sent for Phillip Miller's ponderous Gardeners' Dictionary. Among th books from England are John Ball's notes on th flora of th Peruvian Andes and on Patagonia.

I take one German lesson a week. Will write again as time permits. Bis dahin, leben Sie wohl!

Yours as ever,

L. H. Bailey, Jr.

Michigan Agricultural College,

DEPARTMENT OF HORTICULTURE AND LANDSCAPE GARDENING.

Agricultural College P. O.
Ingham Co., Mich., May 23 1887.

My Dear Deane:

I don't think that I can secure leaves from many if any of the trees from which I secured the popls. catkins last year. Look at the buds. They are fully as characteristic as the leaves. Although P. grandidentata is common here I have never found a pistillate tree low enough to enable me to get fruit. Last year a very tall tree was cut down on the campus and from that I secured the fruit I sent you. I will look up my specimens of poplars and so far as I can identify the trees, will secure lvs.

I have not a sprig of Salix tristis in my herb. Never saw it.

Fine weather. Yours &c

L. H. Bailey, Jr.

Michigan Agricultural College,

COLLEGE FACULTY:

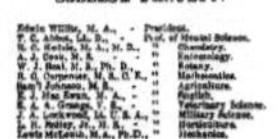

DEPARTMENT OF HORTICULTURE AND LANDSCAPE GARDENING.

Agricultural College P. O.,

Ingham Co., Mich., May 26 1887

My Dear Deane:

When you are at the Gardens again please look at Robinia hispida and see if any of the specimens have seeds. In a French book, which I am reading, I find the statement that it never produces seeds, either in Europe or America.

I have also another favor to ask. In Dr Goodale's Botany, p. 458, note, a reference is made to a paper on the influence of foreign pollen on fruit by Maximowicz. If not too much trouble, will you please look it up and see how extensive a paper it is and in what language. If it is worth having I will send abroad for it.

Michigan Agricultural College,

DEPARTMENT OF HORTICULTURE AND LANDSCAPE GARDENING.

Agricultural College P. O.,
Ingham Co., Mich., June 6 1885

My Dear Deane:

I send you by this mail a few plants, some of which may be interesting to you. I think that I sent you the Plantago once before with a name that I rec'd from Dr Gray. At any rate I sent a specimen to Dr Gray and he named it for me, but somehow I failed to enter the name on my specimen. I did the same with a composite, a Hypochoeris. Sometime when you are at the Herb. look at Hypochoeris please, and see if my specimen is preserved there and what it is named. I think it is H. radicata. I have but one spec. left.

Michigan Agricultural College,

DEPARTMENT OF HORTICULTURE AND LANDSCAPE GARDENING.

Agricultural College P. O., Ingham Co., Mich., 188

Thanks for the little Acira. The Carex sent in yours of the 30th ult. is C. stricta. Put your glass on the buds of the poplars. In P. grand. they are hairy, fat, &c; in P. trem. smooth, sticky, slim, &c. Yes, I should like Salix nigra var. falcata. You must have had a delightful time at the Old Manse.

I do not wish to impose upon you any more, but if you go up to Waverley before long I wish you would look for Carex retrocurva Dewey, for me. I found much of it there once. I turned to the right just beyond some School or asylum (about which are so many Pinus rigida, and a retaining wall in front), and went up the hill until I came to the first house on the left. There I procured a glass of milk which enabled me to go into the dell ~~[illegible]~~ towards the left of the house and to find the Carex growing just back of a field and not far from the highway. It grows in dense glaucous-blue stools, and is very conspicuous. If you should happen to run across it and can do so conveniently, please get me a root to plant. Notice whether the culms stand up or recline on the ground. I also want more herb. specimens. Now you must not go up on purpose for it, but if you happen in ~~that~~ vicinity, just look for it.

Yours Truly,

L. H. Bailey, Jr.

Yes, the No. 5 is Carex monile. Will be in good condition in a week or so. Should like some of the C. vulgaris and a spec. of the Pogonia. Thanks for the Dr Jekyll & Mr. Hyde.

Hot.

I am glad that the plants interested you.

The C. rosea var. is very good.

Coll., June 13 –

L. H. B. Jr.

UNITED STATES
POSTAL CARD.
NOTHING BUT THE ADDRESS TO BE ON THIS SIDE.
Walter Deane,
Brewster Place,
Cambridge, Mass.

Dear D—

No. 1. = C. vulgaris evidently

" 2. = C. straminea var. aperta Boott.

" 3. = C. canescens —

" 4. = C. panicea.

The Carex from Belmont, growing in tufts, is C. . . . .

The Dorchester Carex is C. . . . .

Never found C. grisea in Mass. Yours

L. H. [illegible] Jr.

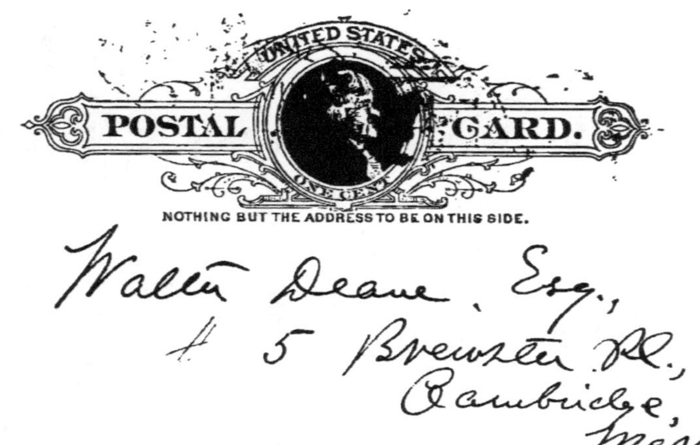
UNITED STATES
POSTAL CARD.
ONE CENT
NOTHING BUT THE ADDRESS TO BE ON THIS SIDE.
Walter Deane, Esq.,
5 Brewster Pl.,
Cambridge,
Mass.

Dear Deane:

Can you not get some flowers from that Catalpa by the old Waterhouse place by the common? It is true C. bignonioides, I think. I have fruit from it. I will press fls. of C. speciosa for you.

Yours, L. H. B. J.

Walter Deane,

Brewster Place,

Cambridge, Mass.

Agric. College
Mich.
June 18, 1887.

Dear D.

9 = C. stricta Lam., the spikes attenuated below.

10 = C. stricta Lam., ordinary form.

I don't think that I shall need any specimens of the above, as they are both common here. Thanks.

L. H. Bailey, Jr.

Walter Deane Esq.
5 Brewster Pl.
Cambridge,
Mass.

June 23

Dear D.

Careosdistans is introduced. I did not know of its occurrence in this country when I wrote the synopsis. I wrote you concerning it sometime ago. It should be no. 152 a in synopsis.

L. H. B. Jr.

UNITED STATES
POSTAL CARD.
NOTHING BUT THE ADDRESS TO BE ON THIS SIDE.
Walter Deane,
Brewster Place,
Cambridge, Mass.

Michigan Agricultural College,

DEPARTMENT OF HORTICULTURE AND LANDSCAPE GARDENING.

Agricultural College P. O.,
Ingham Co., Mich., June 26 1887

My Dear D:

You will please accept thanks for the replies to my numerous questions, also for the Carex scirpoides.

The Carex season is nearly over here now. It is surprising that Carices which are very abundant in Massachusetts should be rare or wanting here. For three years I have looked here for C. scoparia, and never found a sprig of it until last Sunday. You know how common it is at Cambridge. C. tribuloides is comparatively rare here, and I have never seen C. tentaculata

Michigan Agricultural College,

DEPARTMENT OF HORTICULTURE AND LANDSCAPE GARDENING.

Agricultural College P. O.
Ingham Co., Mich., July 6 1887

My Dear Deane:

Yes, the Carices are C. Grayi and squarrosa. Must be waifs.

I did not mean to say that Carices are not common here. On the contrary we have over 60 species close about here. But some common Eastern species are wanting.

I am very busy now with many details, and I give one lecture a day.

Yesterday I found Vitis cordifolia, the first time found in Michigan.

Yours as ever,
L. H. Bailey, Jr.

Happy vacation!

Michigan Agricultural College,

COLLEGE FACULTY:

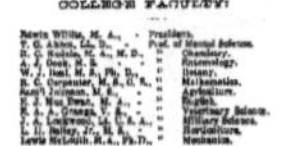

DEPARTMENT OF HORTICULTURE AND LANDSCAPE GARDENING.

Agricultural College, P. O.,
Ingham Co., Mich., July 15 1887

My Dear Deane:

The Carices which you sent from Concord in your letter of the 8th inst. are CC. riparia and siccata. The grass must be Poa serotina. It varies much. The Sedum I take to be the common S. Telephium.

I have also your letter of the 11th. from Cambridge. I shall be very glad of the Catalpa and Salices.

You are having a delightful vacation. I should like to be with you.

Yours in haste,

L. H. Bailey, Jr.

Michigan Agricultural College,

COLLEGE FACULTY:

Edwin Willits, M. A.,	President.
T. C. Abbot, LL. D.,	Prof. of Mental Science.
R. C. Kedzie, M. A., M. D.,	" Chemistry.
A. J. Cook, M. S.,	" Entomology.
W. J. Beal, M. S., Ph. D.,	" Botany.
R. C. Carpenter, M. S., C. E.,	" Mathematics.
Sam'l Johnson, M. S.,	" Agriculture.
E. J. MacEwan, M. A.,	" English.
E. A. A. Grange, V. S.,	" Veterinary Science.
J. A. Lockwood, Lt. U. S. A.,	" Military Science.
L. H. Bailey, Jr., M. S.,	" Horticulture.
Lewis McLouth, M. A., Ph. D.,	" Mechanics.

DEPARTMENT OF HORTICULTURE AND LANDSCAPE GARDENING.

Agricultural College P. O.,

Ingham Co., Mich., July 24 1887

My Dear Deane:

I have your two cards from Nantucket and the letter containing the carices. One carex is C. filiformis as you suppose, and the other appears to be true C. vulgaris, but it is badly shattered.

You are finding many good things and I shall be very glad to get a share of them. Scarcely any of them are represented in my herb. and none sufficiently.

If I wish to make a name to mean stricta-like, shall I write it strictioides?

Our very hot weather has caught an agreeable cold. I am doing almost no botanizing now. I am very busy.

You are having a delightful time.

Yours ever, L. H. Bailey, Jr.

State Horticultural Society.

Annual Membership, $1.00. Life Membership, $10.00.

Home,
July 29 1887.

My Dear Deane:

All last year I mounted very few Carices. I had so many other things on my hands that I could not. But this summer I have taken odd minutes to mount what I could. I am now almost caught up. I have kept track of how many I have put into my herb. at each time. This morning I added up and found that I have put in 601 new specimens, largely new sheets. A careful estimate reveals the fact that I have some 1300 sheets in my herb., averaging two labels to a

OFFICERS

PRESIDENT,
T. T. Lyon, South Haven

SECRETARY,
Chas. W. Garfield, Grand Rapids.

TREASURER,
S. M. Pearsall, Grand Rapids.

LIBRARIAN,
Thos. H. Forster, Lansing.

EXECUTIVE BOARD.
W. K. Gibson, Jackson.
H. W. Davis, Lapeer.
L. H. Bailey, Jr., Ag'l Coll.
A. G. Gulley, South Haven.
E. H. Scott, Ann Arbor.
C. A. Sessions, Mears.

MICHIGAN
State Horticultural Society.

Annual Membership, $1.00. Life Membership, $10.00.

1887.

sheet, making a total of 2600 mounted specimens of carices. Aside from these I have many from Europe, New Zealand, etc. This is not a bad showing for four years work when the matter is entirely a side issue with me. It is my play, simply. I average, you see, 9 sheets to a species.

Were it not for the fact that the collections in Herb. Gray and Herb. Torr. contain so many historic specimens I should prefer my collection to any in the country.

I hope that you are still enjoying yourselves.

Yours as ever, L. H. Bailey, Jr.

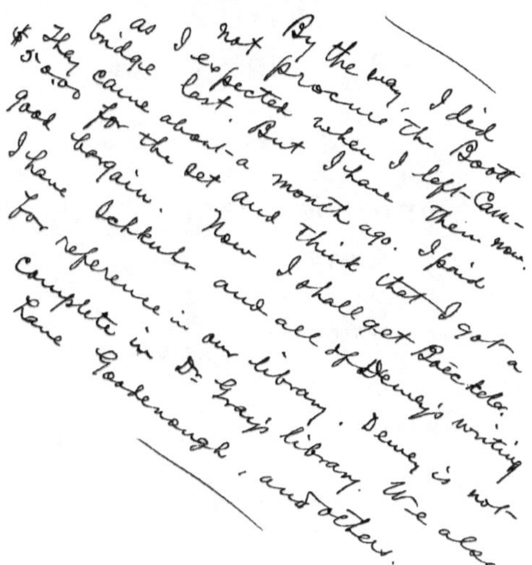

By the way, I did not procure the Boott as I expected when I left Cambridge last. But I have them now. * They came about a month ago. I paid $5.00 for the set and think that I got a good bargain. Now I shall get Boeckeler. I have Schkuhr and all of Dewey's writing for reference in our library. Dewey is not complete in Dr. Gray's library. We also have Goodenough, and others.

MICHIGAN

State Agricultural College.

Program

FOR

Commencement Week

AUGUST 12-17, 1887.

FRIDAY, AUGUST 12, 6 P. M.,
Military Exercises.

FRIDAY, 12th, }
MONDAY, 15th, } 8 P. M.,
Society Banquets.

SUNDAY, AUGUST 14, 2:30 P. M.
President Willits's Baccalaureate Address.

SUNDAY, AUGUST 14, 7:30 P. M.,
Address before the Y. M. C. A.

TUESDAY, AUGUST 16, 8 P. M.,
Class Day Exercises.

WEDNESDAY, AUGUST 17, 10 A. M.,
Graduating Exercises.

WEDNESDAY, AUGUST 17, 8 to 10 P. M.,
President's Reception.

Walter Deane
Brewster Place,
Cambridge, Mass.

Michigan Agricultural College,

COLLEGE FACULTY:

DEPARTMENT OF HORTICULTURE AND LANDSCAPE GARDENING.

Agricultural College P. O.,
Ingham Co., Mich., Aug 14 1887

My Dear Deane:

My term work closed day before yesterday, and now I am free for ten days. I never worked so hard as I have this summer, and I am pretty well tired out.

Tuesday night I go to Chicago to spend a week in the parks and gardens. As soon as I return I begin a course of lectures on horticulture which will keep me very busy.

I have done almost no botanical work of late. I collect none. In fact, there is no use of trying to collect as vegetation is exceedingly parched with drouth. I never knew a drier summer. The best respite I have had during the summer was a half days ride and botanizing with the famous A. R. Wallace of England, author of "Island Life" and other remarkable volumes.

I have a very fine collection of Carices

Michigan Agricultural College,

COLLEGE FACULTY:

DEPARTMENT OF HORTICULTURE AND LANDSCAPE GARDENING.

Agricultural College P. O.,

Ingham Co., Mich.,....................188....

from the White Mts. Collected by Edwin Faxon.

Before long I hope to get time to study some new Carex material I have and to make another paper for the Gazette.

I shall await your bundle with interest.

Yours truly,
L. H. Bailey, Jr.

THE GRAND PACIFIC HOTEL.
DRAKE, PARKER & CO. PROPRIETORS.

Chicago, Aug 28 1887

My Dear Deane:

I am having a delightful vacation in the city. The Society of American Florists is in session here and I am in attendance. The meeting closes to-night but I shall remain in the city until Sunday night. Our term opens Monday night.

My principal business here is the interviewing of prominent experimenting Florists as to how new varieties of flowers are produced. I am learning much,

THE GRAND PACIFIC HOTEL.

DRAKE, PARKER & CO. PROPRIETORS.

Chicago. 188

yet I am surprised to find that even the best of them know little of the scientific aspects of the case.

After the Society adjourned I shall spend my time in the parks and gardens of the city. I have a photographic outfit with me, and I shall take pictures.

Hope that you are still having a good time. Regards to Mrs. Sewall.

Yours as ever,

L. H. Bailey, Jr.

Michigan Agricultural College,

COLLEGE FACULTY:

[illegible]

DEPARTMENT OF HORTICULTURE AND LANDSCAPE GARDENING.

Agricultural College P. O.

Ingham Co., Mich., Sept. 9 1887.

My Dear Deane:

Your pleasant letter of the 5th from York reminds me again that I am debtor in this pleasant correspondence. It seems that as the years roll their weight upon one work increases also. I have never had so much to do and so much to distract me as I have of late. Your vacation is drawing to a close. I am better off than you: I am looking forward to mine. This winter I shall stay at home and study. I hope to get caught up a little. I accomplished very little last winter.

I am much obliged for the seeds of the Smilacinas. Although I have fct. of both, I never before saw the seeds. They are odd enough.

I fear that I cannot get you good Aster

Michigan Agricultural College,

COLLEGE FACULTY:

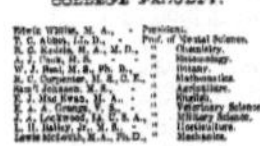

DEPARTMENT OF HORTICULTURE AND LANDSCAPE GARDENING.

Agricultural College P.O.,

Ingham Co., Mich., ...188...

juncea as the season has been so very dry that the Composites make little show. We are having good rains now, and if frost holds off I may be able to find some. The others, the Solidagos and Asters, about which you enquire, do not grow here. Polygala verticillata grows here but is not common. Would like a specimen if you have it to spare.

Remember us both to Mrs. Deane.

Yours as ever,

L. H. Bailey, Jr.

Michigan Agricultural College,

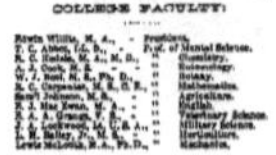

DEPARTMENT OF HORTICULTURE AND LANDSCAPE GARDENING.

Agricultural College P. O.,
Ingham Co., Mich. Sept. 14 1887

My Dear Deane:

Enclosed please find a picture which I found

Yours as ever,
L. H. Bailey, Jr.

Hibbard House,

CLARK & ...

Jackson, Mich. Sept. 20 1887

My Dear Deane:

I rec'd your card saying that your vacation had nearly drawn to a close. I do not know whether to write congratulations or regrets. In ~~ma~~ my own case, I tire of the long vacation before it is over and long for the business of school time. I presume the case is different with you, however, for your vacation is spent among such delightful scenes that you can not help regretting to leave them.

I am in the cozy little city of Jackson this week, in attendance at the State Fair; or, rather, I am working in the capacity of an officer of the same. Michigan has long been famous for the excellence of her fruit displays, and this year, although excessively dry, is no exception. Of all those who exhibit, your humble servant, as a representative of the college and county, has the largest exhibition!

Wife and baby were well when I left them yesterday morning. That baby is one of the brightest girls anyone ever saw. She has been with us since the 29th of last June, and she persists, at the present time, in weighing 18 pounds.

Yours truly,

L. H. Bailey, Jr.

Michigan Agricultural College,

HORTICULTURAL DEPARTMENT.

Agricultural College, P. O.,
Ingham Co., Mich., Oct. 11 1887

My Dear Deane:

In your card of the 4th inst. you did not give me the address of Mrs. E. B. Kendrick to whom you wish me to send a Carex Synopsis. I will gladly send her one. I fully agree with you in wanting many specimens of a plant. One can never know a species well from one or two specimens. It has been many weeks now since I have any more than looked into my herbarium, and I am beginning to feel lonesome. The cold rainy days are coming, however, presaging a close of outside operations and suggesting the pleasures of the snug herbarium. I shall be very glad of all the interesting specimens which you promise me. Of course I am in no hurry for them, for it will still be some time before I get actively at work in my herbarium.

The baby's picture was taken when

Michigan Agricultural College,

HORTICULTURAL DEPARTMENT.

Agricultural College P. O.,

Ingham Co., Mich., ...188...

She was 9 weeks old. She is the most advanced child of her age I ever saw. She begins to laugh and play, and is very interesting. She is the best specimen I have got, by all means.

We are all well.

Let me hear from you often.

Yours as ever,

L. H. Bailey, Jr.

The Ebbitt:

F. C. WILLARD, PROP.

Washington, D. C., Oct. 16, 1887.

My Dear Deane:

How satisfying is the knowledge of plants to one in any city or in any mood of mind! How quickly a new species obtrudes itself upon the traveller and recalls pleasant associations or gives promise of new acquaintances! One may know all the species of any region through manual descriptions, yet he is not acquainted with them until he sees the plants themselves growing naturally. Even good herbarium specimens can give no adequate idea of the larger plants. What a mere travesty, at best, is the fragmentary sheet of magnolia as compared with the glossy-leafed tree which now presents its great cones of fruit in Lafayette Square! There is, to be sure, great satisfaction in the herbarium, but I find that my greatest satisfaction in it comes when winter covers nature's great herbarium, when the woods are leafless and every herb is hidden beneath the frozen earth. Then I find a snug, cozy comfort among my plants, and I can study and compare the floras of widely different places almost at a glance. But the true knowledge of plants comes only when one knows them as they are, as they grow. All the inspirations of novelty of scene, of peculiarity of habit, and of contrast with familiar forms crowd upon one so rapidly that he dances in mental delight.

Yours sincerely, L. H. Bailey, Jr.

The Ebbitt:

C. C. WILLARD, PROP.

Washington, D. C., Oct. 19, 1887

My Dear Deane:

Would that I were coming to Cambridge, but next Saturday will find me at home, D.V.

I came here last Saturday to attend a meeting of the representatives of Agricultural Colleges and experiment stations, a convention which is now in session. It is a very important convention being largely composed of college presidents. It was with considerable trepidation that your humble servant yesterday his voice in so important a conclave. However, I survived, and I shall probably repeat the experiment.

I had once thought of coming to Cambridge this winter but I now see no way of doing so. The baby is too young to make the journey, and with lectures, and no end of other work, I can not see my way clear to leave.

The President of Cornell desires that I give a course of lectures before that institution this winter. Should I accept — as I probably shall not, — however, — I shall need to put every available minute into preparation.

Regards to Mrs. D.

Yours as ever,

L. H. Bailey, Jr.

Michigan Agricultural College,

COLLEGE FACULTY:

HORTICULTURAL DEPARTMENT.

Agricultural College P. O.,

Ingham Co., Mich., Nov. 4 1887

My Dear Deane:

I am very much obliged for the pockets of fruit you sent me and, in anticipation, for the nice specimens which I am to receive, and which are just what my herbarium needs.

Yes, I am getting many carices, but the travelling collectors seldom send more than one specimen of a kind. However, I have a number for you, which I will send with the carices which you said you had for me to determine.

When you have time I want you to do an errand for me at the Gardens. I want cuttings from the various Ribes there. You know where the bushes are. I want cuttings of the length of this year's growth, or about a foot long, 10 or 12 of each except Ribes rubrum.

Michigan Agricultural College,

HORTICULTURAL DEPARTMENT.

Agricultural College, P. O.,

Ingham Co., Mich.,.............. 188..

I want them for planting. I once wrote to Dr Goodale for them but never heard from him. I suppose he overlooked the matter. Of course I am in no hurry for them.

The baby is getting very interesting. We call her Sara May.

Yours truly

L. H. Bailey, Jr.

Michigan Agricultural College,

COLLEGE FACULTY:

DEPARTMENT OF HORTICULTURE AND LANDSCAPE GARDENING.

Agricultural College P. O.,

Ingham Co., Mich., Nov. 13 1887.

My Dear Deane:

Thanks for the fruits.

Mr. Arthur must have sent you the report on our Northern trip. You have before this no doubt rec'd one from me, which you can give to some friend.

Dr. Beal asks $2.50 for his grass book. Perhaps I can get it cheaper for you. Will see. I doubt if you would care so much for this volume as it treats mostly of the agri-cultural phase of the question. Still it has some excellent morphology. He is now at work on the second volume, which is to be a de-scription of all N. American grasses. That you will want.

Yours &c

L.H.B., Jr.

School is out!

Bairn has two teeth.

Thanks for the pockets of fruits.

Michigan Agricultural College,

HORTICULTURAL DEPARTMENT.

Agricultural College P. O.,
Ingham Co., Mich., Nov. 20, 1887

My Dear Deane:

How can I ever repay you for 120 species of plants! That is a good many. I shall look for them with interest.

Our first snow of any account is now falling. It is 3 in. deep on the level. Shall drive to town with a cutter in the morning. School has been closed over a week and everything is very quiet up here. One of our professors has gone to California and our president goes in a day or two. The rest of us will stay here this winter. I shall be away more or less all winter. I have an appointment, with good pay, to give a course of lectures at Cornell University this winter. Do not know yet as I shall go.

I am glad to hear that Larrabee is improving. He must be in an interesting plant region.

Yours L. H. Bailey, Jr.

Agricultural College, Mich.,
Nov. 2d, 1887

My Dear Deane:

I am teasing up the carices again, and by spring you will probably have an abundance of work in straightening out your specimens. Something is the matter with C. canescens, this time. I am becoming convinced that our plant is not the var. alpicola of Wall., but that that name should be applied to the very dwarf and singular form of the White and Rocky Mts., which, I am convinced, is a distinct variety. Now sometime when you are at the Gardens please look in Andersson's Cyperaceae (under A in library) and see when and where Laestadius published his var. subloliacea of C. canescens, and send me just the short Latin characterization of it. I shall procure specimens of it, also.

I have been making a critical comparison of our so-called C. frigida with European specimens, and find, what I have always suspected, that our plant is not the same as the European. I shall separate it as C. ablata.

Seriously, however, I hope I shall not make any more confusion, but some points need to be straightened out in a short paper.

Did I tell you that Dr Gray has sent me Boeckeler's writings on Carex, also Dr Boott's own copy of the Carices of Hook. Fl. Bor.-Am.? They were Wm. Boott's copies.

Yours as ever,

L. H. Bailey, Jr.

Michigan Agricultural College,

COLLEGE FACULTY:

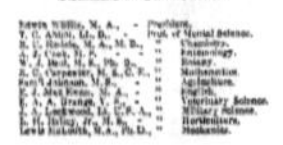

DEPARTMENT OF HORTICULTURE AND LANDSCAPE GARDENING.

Agricultural College P.O.,

Ingham Co., Mich., Nov. 30 1887

My Dear Deane:

The plants and your letter are at hand. I am delighted with the plants, both on account of the number of specimens and their excellent condition. They are perfect, and I can appreciate the pains you have taken with them. I hardly know how to thank you for them. My collections have been few and poor this year, and I have little to offer you. The plants carried nicely in the sheets. I have not looked them over critically yet.

I have finally decided to accept the appointment to lecture to the

Michigan Agricultural College,

COLLEGE FACULTY:

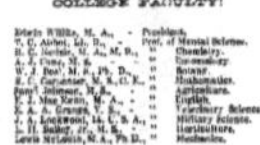

DEPARTMENT OF HORTICULTURE AND LANDSCAPE GARDENING.

Agricultural College P.O.

Ingham Co., Mich. 188..

Seniors at Cornell three or four times a week for Jan. 4 to Jan. 20. They offered me $500.00 for it, and I could not resist.

Next week I go to Saginaw to the annual meeting of the State Hort. Socy. I shall be away more or less at institutes in Mich. and N.Y. Have delivered two lectures already this vacation. My vacation does not mean rest, you see.

Accept my best thanks for the very excellent plants.

Yours as ever,

L. H. Bailey

Michigan Agricultural College,

HORTICULTURAL DEPARTMENT.

Agricultural College P. O.,
Ingham Co., Mich., Dec. 3 1887

My Dear Deane:

Yes, that is right about the Ribes. College pays for it.

I have enjoyed the picture of ferns very much. Have studied them all out under my glass. Thanks.

Have just procured Drejer's Symbolae Caricologicae and Liebmann's Mexicos Halvgraes.

Yours in a hurry,
L. H. B.

Michigan Agricultural College,

COLLEGE FACULTY:

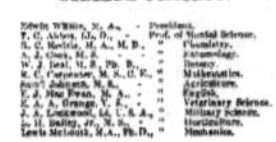

DEPARTMENT OF HORTICULTURE AND LANDSCAPE GARDENING.

Agricultural College P. O.,
Ingham Co., Mich., Dec. 10 1887

My Dear Deane:

Upon returning from Saginaw last night I found your postal and letter. The sad news has almost made me sick. It is on my mind all the time. It is almost like a family bereavement to me. I can have no hope for recovery from such condition as you describe, and I cannot bear the thought that I shall never see the kind and genial face again. Do keep me posted. I shall look for your next letter with mingled hope and dread.

Yours Truly,
L. H. Bailey, Jr.

Michigan Agricultural College,

HORTICULTURAL DEPARTMENT.

Agricultural College, P. O.,
Ingham Co., Mich., Dec. 11 1887

My Dear Deane:

I am under great obligations to you for your daily information concerning Dr Gray. I am gathering much hope for his ultimate recovery, although I fear that he can never prosecute his labor to any extent again. Yet we must hope for the best. It is all very sad.

I will look up the matter of Dr Beal's book as soon as I get time.

I have put into my herb. all the plants which you have sent except those which I am to examine. They are a fine lot, and I appreciate them, I assure you. Of course I already had many of them, but they are just as acceptable for all that. I am more and more impressed with the necessity of having several specimens of each species and variety.

Yours as ever, L. H. Bailey, Jr.

The cuttings are here in good condition. Thanks.

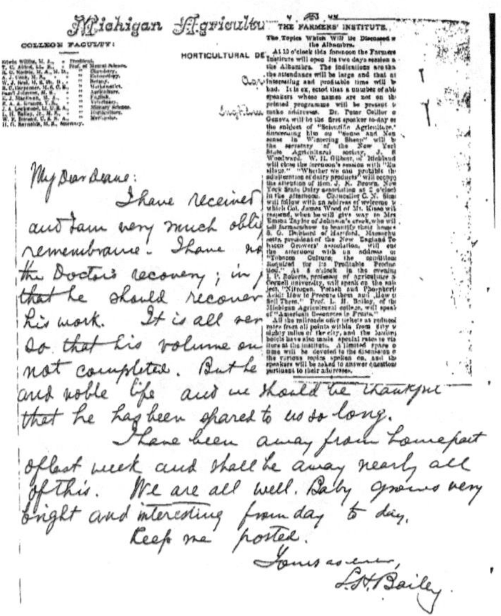

Michigan Agricultu[...]

COLLEGE FACULTY:

HORTICULTURAL DE[...]

My Dear Deane:

I have received [...]
and I am very much obli[...]
remembrance. I have n[...]
the Doctor's recovery; in [...]
that he should recover [...]
his work. It is all ver[...]
so that his volume on [...]
not completed. But he [...]
and noble life and we should be thankful
that he has been spared to us so long.

I have been away from home part
of last week and shall be away nearly all
of this. We are all well. Baby grows very
bright and interesting from day to day.

Keep me posted.

Yours as ever,

L. H. Bailey.

THE FARMERS' INSTITUTE.

The Topics Which Will Be Discussed [a]t the Alhambra.

At 10 o'clock this forenoon the Farmers' Institute will open its two days session at the Alhambra. The indications are that the attendance will be large and that an interesting and profitable time will be had. It is expected that a number of able speakers whose names are not on the printed programme will be present to make addresses. Dr. Peter Collier of Geneva will be the first speaker to-day on the subject of "Scientific Agriculture." Succeeding him on "Sense and Nonsense in Wintering Sheep" will be the secretary of the New York State Agricultural society, J. S. Woodward. W. H. Gilbert, of Richland will close the forenoon's session with "Ensilage." "Whether we can prohibit the adulteration of dairy products" will occupy the attention of Hon. J. K. Brown, New York State Dairy association at 2 o'clock in the afternoon. Chancellor C. N. Sims will follow with an address of welcome to which Col. James Wood of Mt. Kisco will respond, when he will give way to Mrs. Emma Taylor of Johnson's creek, who will tell farmers how to beautify their homes. S. G. Hubbard of Hartford, Massachusetts, president of the New England Tobacco Growers' association, will end the afternoon with an address on "Tobacco Culture; the Conditions Required for its Profitable Production." At 8 o'clock in the evening I. P. Roberts, professor of agriculture at Cornell university, will speak on the subject, "Nitrogen, Potash and Phosphoric Acid: How to Procure them and How to Sell Them." Prof. L. H. Bailey, of the Michigan Agricultural college, will speak of "American Grownees in Fruits."

All the railroads offer tickets at reduced rates from all points within from fifty to eighty miles of the city, and the leading hotels have also made special rates to visitors at the institute. A limited space of time will be devoted to the discussion of the various topics spoken on, and the speakers will be asked to answer questions pertinent to their addresses.

Michigan Agricultural College,

HORTICULTURAL DEPARTMENT.

Agricultural College P. O.,
Ingham Co., Mich., Dec. 18 1887

My Dear Deane:

I have received your daily bulletins and I am very much obliged to you for your remembrance. I have now given up all hope of the Doctor's recovery; in fact I cannot wish that he should recover if he cannot continue his work. It is all very sad, and the more so that his volume on the Polypetalae was not completed. But he has had a long and noble life and we should be thankful that he has been spared to us so long.

I have been away from home part of last week and shall be away nearly all of this. We are all well. Baby grows very bright and interesting from day to day.

Keep me posted.

Yours as ever,

L. H. Bailey.

Syracuse, N.Y., Dec. 20, '87

My Dear Deane:

I sent you by express (paid) yesterday a small bundle of plants. I am sorry that I had no more to send you. I may have a few carices to send you towards spring.

As I am not posted on sedges outside of Carex, I did not put my name on the labels of the Cyperus, etc. I think ~~that~~ they are correct, however. Your Rhynchospora is evidently R. plumosa, as you suppose.

The Eriophorum is simply

proliferous, as Allium Canadense sometimes is. Your Catalpa is good C. bignonioides.

The Cercis which I send is from the same tree as the flowering specimen which I sent you last spring. Destroy the former label, for the one I send will answer for both.

I enclosed 3 plants — an Alyssum & two Physalises — for determination sometime. I am in no manner of hurry for the names, and I doubt if you can make much of the Physalis. Don't bother much with them. I sent some to Dr. Gray a few weeks ago but he never got to them. I presume that they are not correctly named.

The enclosed excerpt will explain why I am here. I expect that the convention will be a notable one.

Yours truly,

L. H. Bailey, Jr.

The Spencer House is the only First-Class Hotel at Niagara Falls open summer and winter, and combines all the elegance of a modern hotel with the quietness and comfort of a home. Its table has always been distinguished for its excellence, and its apartments are the best ventilated and most commodious at Niagara.

Spencer House, Niagara Falls, N. Y.

Dec. 23, 1887

My Dear Deane:

I have given many lectures and talks off and on, but I never made such an impression upon my hearers as I made recently at Albion. I am now pretty well fagged out, and shall be glad enough to see wife and baby to-morrow afternoon.

I have seen nothing in the papers concerning Dr Gray, so that I suppose ~~that~~ he still lives. I shall receive news from you when I get home.

Merry Christmas to you and yours.

Yours truly, L. H. Bailey

MICHIGAN
STATE
Horticultural Society.

VICE-PRESIDENT'S OFFICE.

Annual Membership, \$1.00. Life Membership, \$10.00.

Lansing, Mich., Dec. 27 1887

My Dear Deane:

Upon arriving at home Saturday I found the pictures of the ferns, for which you will please accept thanks. They are very nice.

You ought to write a catalogue of Cambridge plants. No one else has so complete a collection of the flora of that vicinity as yourself. The Boston Natural Hist. Soc., or some other organization, would publish it for you.

A week from to-day I start

for New York again, this time to remain chiefly at Cornell.

Happy New Year from us both.

Yours ever,

L. H. Bailey, Jr.

I am very thankful for your postals concerning Dr. Gray. I look for them with eagerness every day.

Niagara Falls, Ontario,
Jan. 3, '88,

My Dear [illegible]:

Address me at Ithaca, N.Y. I shall be anxious, as usual, to hear about Dr. Gray. This time I am taking in the Falls from a Canadian standpoint. Although the scenery is fine from this side, the manners & customs are not. I have always found this so. Too "English" for me. Reach Cornell to-night. Regards to Mrs. D. Yours

L. H. B. J.

Walter Deane,
Brewster Place,
Cambridge, Mass.

Michigan Agricultural College,

DEPARTMENT OF HORTICULTURE AND LANDSCAPE GARDENING.

~~Agricultural College, P. O.~~
Ithaca, N. Y. ~~Ingham Co. Mich.~~ Jan. 8 1888

My Dear Deane:

I received this morning your card of the 2nd., which had been forwarded. It is the first news of Dr Gray since I came here. How long he lingers!

I am getting well into my work, having already delivered three lectures. This is a great institution, and it will soon be among the foremost of Universities. They claim 1000 students in attendance now. The buildings are numerous and very fine and the equipments excellent. The University occupies a commanding site, some over 400 feet above Cayuga lake and the village of Ithaca. The campus is bounded on two sides by wild and picturesque gorges through which water plunges with

Michigan Agricultural College,

COLLEGE FACULTY:

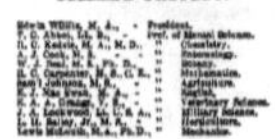

DEPARTMENT OF HORTICULTURE AND LANDSCAPE GARDENING.

Agricultural College P. O.

Ingham Co., Mich.......... ....188..

fury over numberless cascades. One of the gorges is 150 feet deep, cut in the rock by time and water, the precipitous and castellated walls being highly picturesque. Fall creek, a considerable stream, plunges through this chasm, falling over two precipices some twenty feet high, and finally tumbles headlong over a wall 110 feet high, and enters the placid lake. The view from the campus is grand. I could never tire of looking far over the undulating hills, dotted with their patchy forests and rolling farms. Cayuga lake, the largest of this parallel sisterhood of lakes, two or three miles broad and forty miles long, winds out of sight in the distance.

Regards to Mrs. B. Yours ...

ITHACA HOTEL.

H. D. FREER, - - Proprietor.

Ithaca, N. Y. Jan. 15 188 8

My Dear Deane:

I am still under great obligations to you and Mrs. Deane for keeping me posted on Dr Gray's condition. How sad it is, now that we know that recovery is impossible, that he should linger so long! But I suppose that he suffers little.

This opens my last week at Cornell. I start home next Friday. So you must not address me here after Wednesday.

I have been at Institutes since last Tuesday. I spent Thursday in New York using there a day which I had between two Conventions. I spent part of the time at the Torrey Herb. among the carices. I had gone over them pretty thoroughly once before. Wednesday I spoke at Middletown, in the S. E. part of the State, and Friday at Sidney, near the headwaters of the Delaware.

I shall be glad enough to get home again. But I shall be there only two or three days when I start out on the Michi-

ITHACA HOTEL.

H. D. FREER, - - Proprietor.

Ithaca, N. Y., Jan. 19 1888

My Dear Deane:

I am astonished at the news from Dr Gray. I am almost building hope that he may recover! How wonderful it would be!

I have now but one more lecture to give. I start home tomorrow night. I can scarcely wait to get home. I was never away so long before.

Yet my stay here has been very profitable. I have been through 200 volumes which we do not have at Lansing, over half of them being French. I have simply read enough of the articles to know if they are of value to me, making record of the fact. Then I shall send here for the books as I need them.

Cornell is a great University, especially considering its age. It is only 20 years old. By the way, I will say to you, _strictly sub rosa_, that I may come here as one of the faculty. I have the chance.

Remember me to Mrs. D. Send the carices at any time.

Yours as ever,

L. H. Bailey

MICHIGAN
State Horticultural Society.

Annual Membership, $1.00. Life Membership, $10.00.

Jan. 29 1888

My Dear Deane:

I arrived home from N.Y. a week ago yesterday, but only staid over Sunday. This last week I have attended a large institute at So. Haven, my old home, and a very successful forestry convention at Grand Rapids. This week I am to remain at home, but next week I am off for the pine woods, where we are to hold a pioneer institute. Wife says that I am making home my headquarters, but live elsewhere. This

the herbarium.

I have not heard from you for some days, so that I suppose Dr Gray has developed no new symptoms. It is very sad that he should linger so long.

We have nice sleighing and not very cold weather. Term opens three weeks from to-morrow, and I begin then a series of lectures to the seniors. I wish that I might hear Dr Goodale in his lecture course.

Baby and mother are well. Regards from us both to yourself and Mrs. Deane.

Yours —

L. H. Bailey

MICHIGAN STATE Horticultural Society.

VICE-PRESIDENT'S OFFICE.

ANNUAL MEMBERSHIP, $1.00. LIFE MEMBERSHIP, $10.00.

Lansing, Mich., Feb. 3 1888

My Dear Deane:

Poor Dr Gray has gone! How strange it seems to me! The last time I saw him he was as bright and cheery as ever, and it hardly seems as if he could die. Surely a great blank is left in the ranks of our botanists and an aching void in the hearts of all who knew him. But he has left a life strewn with roses, and has shed light always. His works are his monument. I can scarcely realize that if I were to step into the herbarium at Cambridge now, I could not see Dr Gray. How thankful I am that I have known him! My life will be the better for such acquaintance.

We are both well. I go to my last institute next week.

Yours as ever,

L. H. Bailey

MICHIGAN STATE Horticultural Society.

VICE-PRESIDENT'S OFFICE.

ANNUAL MEMBERSHIP, $1.00. LIFE MEMBERSHIP, $10.00.

Lansing, Mich., ... 188

As soon as you get time will you please send me the short description of Carex grisea in Wahlenberg's Inledning, 154? C. grisea needs revision very much.

L. H. B.

State Horticultural Society.

Annual Membership, $1.00. Life Membership, $10.00.

Feb. 12 1888.

My Dear Deane:

The package of carices is at hand, but I have not yet had time to name the specimens. I also wish to wait until I hear from you in regard to C. grisea, for I have made a revision for that species, but do not know which form Wahlenberg had. One of those you send is grisea.

During the last week I have attended an institute in the pine woods. Good honest weather up there. 26° below

State Horticultural Society.

Annual Membership, $1.00. Life Membership, $10.00.

1887.

zero the first night — and I rode 7 miles in an open sleigh — and 25° below the second night. It was up pretty well towards the n. of the lower peninsula. All that country is entirely unexplored in a scientific way. The county has less than 4000 people. Dr Beal and myself are planning a two weeks' trip in those great forests for next July.

How lonely the gardens must seem without Dr Gray! I shall almost dread to go there hereafter. How thankful I am that I have known him!

State Horticultural Society.

Annual Membership, $1.00. Life Membership, $10.00.

1887.

College opens the 20th. Then begins business again. Yet I have worked harder during this checkered vacation than I shall during term time.

Yours as ever,

L. H. Bailey.

The Wayne,
OPENED DEC. 1, 1887.
W. P. F. MESERVE, PROP'R.

OPPOSITE M. C. R. R. DEPOT,
FROM WHICH BAGGAGE IS TRANSFERRED WITHOUT CHARGE.
PRICES $2 TO $3.50 PER DAY.

Detroit, Mich., Feb. 8 1888.

My Dear Deane:

I rec'd your note on Carex grisea the first of the week. Thanks.

I left home Tuesday for central New York and Cornell. I shall reach home to-day. I was sent for by the authorities of Cornell, who are pushing pretty hard to persuade me to locate there.

I am getting a little tired of this gadding. All winter I have been on the go. I have had no rest out of my vacation. College opens day after to-morrow and with it opens a year's work. I had hoped to reach Cambridge during some of my peregrinations, but cannot now.

OPENED DEC. 1, 1887.
W. P. F. MESERVE, PROP'R.

OPPOSITE M. C. R. R. DEPOT,
FROM WHICH BAGGAGE IS TRANSFERRED WITHOUT CHARGE.

PRICES $2 TO $3.50 PER DAY.

Detroit, Mich. 1888.

The [illegible] studies which I have deferred for the last year and more were mostly completed before I left, and my MS. is now in Printer's hands.

Let me hear from you oftener.

Yours ever,

L. H. Bailey

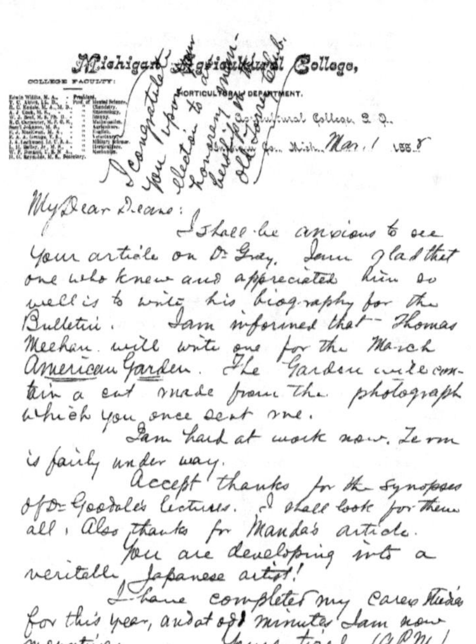

Michigan Agricultural College,

COLLEGE FACULTY:

HORTICULTURAL DEPARTMENT.

Agricultural College P. O.,
Ingham Co., Mich., Mar. 1 1888

I congratulate you upon your election to honorary membership in the old Torrey Club.

My Dear Deane:

I shall be anxious to see your article on Dr. Gray. I am glad that one who knew and appreciated him so well is to write his biography for the Bulletin. I am informed that Thomas Meehan will write one for the March American Garden. The Garden will contain a cut made from the photograph which you once sent me.

I am hard at work now. Term is fairly under way.

Accept thanks for the synopses of Dr. Goodale's lectures. I shall look for them all. Also thanks for Manda's article.

You are developing into a veritable Japanese artist!

I have completed my Carex studies for this year, and at odd minutes I am now mounting.

Yours, tired, (9 P.M.)

L. H. Bailey

Michigan Agricultural College,

HORTICULTURAL DEPARTMENT.

Agricultural College P. O.,
Ingham Co., Mich., Mar. 8 1888

My Dear Deane:

I am much interested in the lectures of Dr Goodale. Will they be published? I hope so.

I have the Pharmaceutische Rundschau with biography of Dr Gray.

Yes, I will make all necessary corrections in synonymy, and nomenclature in your Carex synopsis. They will be few and such as you can readily make yourself when my next paper appears (March Gazette).

There is no native honey bee, Prof. Cook, says.

You certainly must be happy over your collection of autographs. Did you get one of John Carey?

Beautiful weather. College is opening up well.

Yours as ever,
L. H. Bailey

Michigan Agricultural College,

HORTICULTURAL DEPARTMENT.

Agricultural College P. O.,
Ingham Co., Mich., Mar. 11 1888

My Dear Deane:

Your biography of Dr Gray is exceedingly interesting because it contains so many personal allusions which cannot be obtained by those who write of a man without having known him. The accounts of his European and other trips are the best and most sympathetic which I have seen. I was particularly pleased with the remark that the Universities honored themselves by conferring degrees upon him. The table of contents promises a portrait but there is none with my copy. It must have slipped out in the mails. I shall write for one.

You have undoubtedly seen the fine portrait issued as a Supplement to Garden and Forest. My Garden + Forest came yesterday noon, and last night the portrait was nicely framed and hanging in my parlor.

We are having delightful days which make me long for the opening of Spring. In a month the Hepatica and Erigenia will begin to bloom. Then will follow that long array of charming spring flowers which make our western copses so attractive.

Yours as ever,

L. H. Bailey

State Horticultural Society.

Annual Membership, $1.00. Life Membership, $10.00.

College, Mar. 23, 1888

My Dear Deane:

The photo of Dr Gray is at hand. It is by far the best likeness I ever saw, and I am very much obliged for it. You once asked me for some of my work in photography. I mail you to-day a poor sample. I hope ~~that it~~ will not shock you. You may not believe in nude art.

Your carices are C. echinata v. microstachys and C. straminea v. ~~chloros~~ moniliformis.

The Synopsis is at hand,

State Horticultural Society.

Annual Membership, $1.00. Life Membership, $10.00.

1887.

and I will look it over soon.

Our beautiful weather caught a severe cold day before yesterday, and last night it took sank below zero.

We are all well. Mrs. B. would be remembered to Mrs. Deane.

Yours as ever,

L. H. Bailey

Michigan Agricultural College,

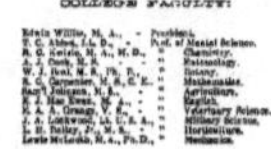

DEPARTMENT OF HORTICULTURE AND LANDSCAPE GARDENING.

Agricultural College P. O.,

Ingham Co., Mich., Mar. 24 1888.

My dear Deane:

In looking over your Synopsis I notice that you lack a few species which I can supply. I accordingly mail you to-day a small parcel, some of the specimens being very poor, however.

Yes, Dr Farlow sent me a copy of his obituary of Tuckerman.

Dewey lived in Rochester the latter part of his life. Write to his son, Chas. Ayrault Dewey, Rochester, N.Y.

I do not know where Carey lived. Dr Gray must have written an obituary of him in Am. Journ. Sci.

Yours as ever,

L. H. Bailey

Michigan Agricultural College,

HORTICULTURAL DEPARTMENT.

Agricultural College P. O.

Ingham Co., Mich. Ap. 4 1888

My Dear Deane:

You will please accept thanks for the determination of the Physalises. I had thought that the "P. edulis" was P. capsicifolia, for I remembered very distinctly the tussle I had over that species at the time you mention.

I am much interested in the synopsis you gave of Dr G's lecture. I have Shenstone's old work, and have taken much pleasure in reading it. Shenstone coined the word "Landscape Gardening".

Mrs. Gray sent me a copy of the memorial.

Spring comes slowly.

I have been discussing the matter of a type-writer but have finally decided that I do not want one.

Yours truly, L. H. Bailey

THE BAILEY HOUSE

L. H. BAILEY & SON. PROP'S

Ionia, Mich. April 11, 1888

My Dear Deane:

Your last letter reach me this morning. Accept thanks for the bulletin on the preservation of wood. I had not seen it.

Is the slip which you enclose a fair same of New England grammar? It is banghing enough.

Our weather holds back remarkably. No spring flowers yet except hazel, which is out in luxuriance.

We are all ordinarily well.

Yours truly,

L. H. Bailey

Agricultural College P. O.

Ingham Co., Mich. Apr. 17 1888

My Dear Deane:

Finally, after many days, the Cornell offer has crystallized itself in my mind, and I have accepted it. It is a full professorship with many perquisites and a season in Europe. Shall not enter actively upon my work there until after the close of our college year in August.

Yours truly,

L. H. Bailey

I return your synopsis.

.·The·Kirkwood.·.

W. D. GIDDINGS,
M. F. BLAINE

GIDDINGS & BLAINE, PROP'RS.

Geneva, N. Y., Apr. 23 1888

My Dear Deane:
Yes, it is true, as you say, that I roam about a good deal. But I can't help it. I roam much more than you know about. My wife says that I belong to the public and not to her any more. I begin to feel that it is so.

Spring is very backward this year. Scarcely anything out yet except a few Hepaticas.

I am tired, but must jog on. I have been

here a half day. Home the last of the week.

As ever,

L. H. Bailey.

Michigan Agricultural College,

HORTICULTURAL DEPARTMENT.

Agricultural College P. O.
Ingham Co., Mich. Apr. 29 1888

My Dear Deane:

Spring is coming on apace. I was out to-day and found abundance of Claytonia, Hepatica, Dentaria ~~diphylla~~ laciniata, Cardamine rotundifolia, Sanguinaria, Erythronium, Dirca, and many willows. Caltha, Erigenia, and others are also out, and Trillium, Caulophyllum and many others will be in bloom in a very few days. Spring is delightful to the botanist in these Michigan fields.

Your C. canescens from Mts. Washn and Willoughby is var. alpicola. That from here is stout var. vulgaris. Probably your Stowe specimens are the same as those from here. Var. vulgaris bears the same relation to C. canescens that

Michigan Agricultural College,

HORTICULTURAL DEPARTMENT.

Agricultural College P. O.,

Ingham Co., Mich. ....188...

In this Country the var. Vulgaris is more common than the species.

You ask what my professorship at Cornell is. It will read "Professor of General and Experimental Horticulture". It is essentially the same as I have here with Landscape Gardening omitted. It is a new chair there. Of course it is closely allied to botany in its scientific aspects, having to do with the whole science of plant growth and variation under culture, such as hybridization, origination of varieties, physiology of healing of wounds, union of grafts, etc., winterkilling, acclimatization, etc etc. In short, it is the most practical and enticing part of botany to me. In a practical way it includes Pomology or fruit culture, Olericulture or vegetable gardening, Floriculture. I shall have an experi-

Michigan Agricultural College,

HORTICULTURAL DEPARTMENT.

Agricultural College P. O.

Ingham Co., Mich. ....188...

is forthcoming. I shall have a gardener and an assistant for class room and laboratory work, with laborers for the Garden. All this I have here but I now have in addition the care of 100 acres of lawn. This is a great burden. At Cornell I can put all my time on professional work. In short, I look upon the place as an ideal one. No institution in America could institute such a department of horticulture as Cornell. The other great Universities have but a very feeble development upon the industrial sides. The nearest approach to my work at Harvard is that done at Bussey, by B. M. Watson.

Some wretch has sent me a postal card with quail* tracks all over the back of it. It may be readable to some folks but it is all Greek to me.

Yours as ever,

L. H. Bailey

CORNELL UNIVERSITY EXPERIMENT STATION,

ITHACA, N. Y.

I. P. ROBERTS, Director. H. H. WING, Deputy Director and Secy. E. L. WILLIAMS, Treasurer.

Horticultural Department.

L. H. BAILEY, Professor of Horticulture.

Agr'l College, Mich., May 11, 1898.

My Dear Deane:

I shall be glad to get fruit of all the plants you mention unless it is the Dirca. That rarely fruits about here, and as I have sold my horse I can not scour the country as heretofore. Already I am beginning to close up my business here. Dirca is now out of flower, I fear, but Sunday I will go into a wood back of my house and see. You asked me to get catkins of Corylus if I could get fruit from the same bush. But as I intend sailing for Europe in August, I cannot get the fruit and hence did not get the flowers.

I showed the quail tracks to our professor of English literature — how a professor of English could ever read it is beyond me — and he gave

CORNELL UNIVERSITY EXPERIMENT STATION,
ITHACA, N. Y.

I. P. ROBERTS, H. H. WING, E. L. WILLIAMS.

Horticultural Department.
L. H. BAILEY, Professor of Horticulture.

189..

utterance to sonorous words of congratulation, for which I am therefore obliged to you. Spring is coming on at a scampering pace and I am head over heels in dirt and delight.

I am leading a most perplexing dual existence — half here, one-fourth about the country in general, and one-fourth at Cornell. I hope to draw the outstanding three quarters to the one Cornell quarter and make up a connected individual again by the opening of another year. If it keeps on in this way I shall have to make a partnership of myself on the plan of Dr. Jekyll and Mr. Hyde.

Baby grows and is very sweet and cunning. Mrs. B. is well and will be remembered to you both.

Yours faithfully,
L. H. Bailey

CORNELL UNIVERSITY EXPERIMENT STATION,
ITHACA, N. Y.

Horticultural Department.

Agric. College, Mich., May 14 1888

My Dear Deane: I am glad that you enjoyed the Shortia. I knew that you would. I had a chance to get the species, so I bought three specimens, one for myself and one for each of my best friends, — Walter Deane and Dr. Beal. Some four or five years ago I had a chance to secure some specimens for $3 apiece but for some reason, which I cannot now recall, I failed to secure them. I did not mean to let another opportunity slip.

You will please accept thanks for the very neat and pleasant reprint of your notice of Dr. Gray.

I have lately completed my mounting of the carices which I decided to keep out of those which came in during last fall and winter, — 275 specimens, — not so many as the year before.

Yours as ever, L. H. Bailey

You have evidently been
taking lessons in free-hand
drawing.

HORTICULTURAL DEPARTMENT.

Agricultural College, Mich.

May 20 1888

My Dear Deane:

You ask for something of my plans in reference to my proposed European trip. It is yet too early to say definitely just what I shall do. I had not intended to go until next year, and to take wife and child, but I have now about decided to go alone for a shorter period. I have come to this decision mostly through my wife's influence. She thinks that I need the rest, and she does not care to go when I go first. You see I took no vacation last winter, when our vacation

Agricultural College, Mich.

..............................188..

occurred, and I am now working hard while Cornell will have its vacation. Thus two years will come together without any vacation. Mrs. B. wants to spend the fall with her mother in Lansing. I really feel much in need of a rest, and will feel more so by the middle of August. Our summer term is a hard one for me. In a few days I am to give a public lecture before faculty and students. June 6 I give an address to a large convention at So. Haven, my birthplace, — a farewell to my old home and my native State — and immeditely there-

Agricultural College, Mich.

3

.................................188

after I speak at the Summer meeting of the State Hort. Socy. Other engagements, which I cannot well escape, are coming on. June 11th I go in company with Dr Beal and C. F. Wheeler (Of the Mich. Catalogue) for that 200-miles trip across the wild pine woods of upper Michigan, from Lake to Lake. It is a singular country, much of it almost unknown. No botanist has ever laid eyes on it! Look on your map and find Alcona Co., on L. Huron. We botanize along the lake at Harrisville, and then plunge into the woods across to Frankfort, in Benzie Co., on L. Michigan! Have I

HORTICULTURAL DEPARTMENT.

Agricultural College, Mich.

4

..........188..

long to be off, to be "near to nature's heart," in the deep, lonely woods and the wild stretches of sandy plains! How happy a man is the botanist, who lives near to nature always!

The summer will pass with an endless chain of duties, and soon will come the alumni reunion of my alma mater, a triennial festival of corpulent dimensions. That will scarcely have passed away when I sail from Quebec on the 24th., on the good ship Circassian, for Londonderry, on the N. coast of Ireland. Then I make a tour of the

Emerald Isle, Scotland, England, Wales, France, Belgium, Holland, Denmark, Germany, Switzerland, Austria (Vienna), Italy, and then a fortnight's cruise in the Adriatic, the shores of Greece, and then a westward course to Boston. Thus do I plan to close a year which began in wandering and which seems destined to be a broken and checkered link in my life. I am not going to Europe to "see sights", nor yet to study. I am going to see gardens, gardeners, herbariums, botanists. I shall pass rapidly, as I must to compass

HORTICULTURAL DEPARTMENT.

Agricultural College, Mich.

6 ..../.............. 188

my design in four months. Incidentally I hope to see the originals of all perplexing American carices. I shall take with me a satchel detective camera, with paper negatives, and shall take pictures by the score.

Now I have tired you all out, and I will stop.

I know Mrs. Britton also. She is very bright.

Yours as ever,
L. H. Bailey

Thanks for Dr. Gray's portrait.

Michigan Agricultural College,

HORTICULTURAL DEPARTMENT.

Agricultural College P. O.

Ingham Co., Mich. May 30 1888.

My Dear Deane: Your pleasant letter of the 27th is at hand. Yes, I will need wings in Europe, but I hope to have them. Of course I have laid out no definite route. I have only indicated what I want to accomplish. But I may not get over nearly so much territory as I am planning for.

I have been indulging a little in a microscope. I have bought a Zentmayer Histological Stand, $40, and have a fine lot of accessories. My objectives range from 3 in to 1/12. The outfit comes to over $300.00, with some back counties yet to hear from.

Prof. W. W. Bailey is a singular man. I have been twice at his house. I like him much. He has a very poor chance at Brown. I, too, have Olney's picture.

Michigan Agricultural College,

HORTICULTURAL DEPARTMENT.

Agricultural College P. O.

Ingham Co., Mich.......... ....188....

I gave my last public lecture before faculty and students to-day. Lectured an hour on pumpkins. These lectures occur once a year for each full professor.

Next week I go to my old home, and week after I am off for the great woods.

The remainder of this week is a great gala day here—3 days. The colleges of Michigan unite here in athletic sports, and hundreds of people will be present. Our grounds are studded with tents, like an army encampment, and I expect nights and days will be alive and aglow with merry-making and trials of skill.

Yours truly,

L. H. Bailey

CORNELL UNIVERSITY EXPERIMENT STATION,
ITHACA, N. Y.

I. P. ROBERTS, Director. H. H. WING, Deputy Director and Sec'y. E. L. WILLIAMS, Treasurer.

Horticultural Department.
L. H. BAILEY, Professor of Horticulture.

Agricultural College, June 9, 1888

My Dear Deane:

Yes, your Carex appears to be C. siccata.

I returned last night from So. Haven, where we had a good time. I addressed an audience of nearly 1000 people. Next Tuesday, June 12th., I start for the woods. You may address here as usual. I will get my mail by messenger.

I am very busy and can not write more now.

Yours Truly,
L. H. Bailey

Seventeenth Annual Meeting

OF THE

VAN BUREN COUNTY PIONEER ASSOCIATION!!

AT

SOUTH HAVEN!!

WEDNESDAY, JUNE 6, 1888.

GOV. C. G. LUCE

Will Deliver an Address from the Grand Stand in the Park,

PRECEDED BY

MUSIC

By the **South Haven Brass Band**, followed with Vocal Music, and also

AN ADDRESS BY

PROF. L. H. BAILEY

And other Noted Speakers.

Arrangements will be made for Reduced Rates on the Railroads, and Trains will be held for the accommodation of those attending from a distance.

This is to be a Social **BASKET PIC-NIC** Occasion, and it is hoped all will bring Full Baskets and pleasant faces for a Royal Good Time.

E. L. WARNER, Sentinel, Secretary. J. J. WOODMAN, President.

In the Woods, June 13, 1888.

My Dear Deane:

Here I am on a bed of hemlock and arbor vitae, watching the coffee on the 'spit', and scribbling a line to you. This morning we plunge into the deep woods. Look at Grayling on your map, and think of us there next Sunday. Two reporters, from two Detroit dailies, accompany us to Grayling. One of our first finds is Carex capillaris!!! I lay last night on mats of C. umbellata. Never saw it growing before. A little way off C. Backii and C. arctata grow abundantly. A singular Carex, evidently a new var. of C. varia, is about us.

I must attend to breakfast.

Yours as ever,

L. H. Bailey

Michigan Horticultural Society

RETURN TO
L. H. BAILEY, Vice-President,
LANSING, - - - - MICH.,
If not called for in ten days.

Walter Deane,
Brewster Place,
Cambridge, Mass.

Mio, Oscoda Co., Mich.,
June 14 '88
8.30 P.M.

My Dear Deane:
Away out of the world I am! I can hardly realize that I am here, in such strange circumstances. Mio, the county seat, and the largest town in the County, contains about 100 people! This County is almost as little known as the plains of Siberia, and yet lumber camps are all through it. All is strange and wild. I have seen scenery which I can never describe. It is grand, yet simple; so lonely, so strange! The primeval forests are beyond all description. We are now on the great interior plains — the home of the jack pine (P. Banksiana) where

large trees never grow
anywhere one can see for
miles in diminutive primeval groves.

We find many inter-
esting plants. Carex vaginata,
C. Houghtonii, C. gynocrates, C. flexilis, and others,
are abundant.

It is now dark and I
must change my photo-
graphic plates. Have taken
already 26 pictures.

Yours &c

F. H. B.

BRACKETT HOUSE

DOPP & STEELE, Prop's

ELEVATOR AND STEAM HEAT.

COMMERCIAL RATE $ 2.00 PER DAY

Rochester N.Y. June 23 1888

My Dear Deane:

My letter this morning will not give you odors of boughs of hemlock nor whifs of great pine woods, yet I feel as if my hands are scarcely free from the smell of the forest in which I was plunged a few hours ago. I enclose you some articles descriptive of our trip. The Free Press reporter left us after two or three days, and I took up his narrative. You will observe that articles 5 & 6 are mine. Another, I expect, appeared in this morning's issue. Of

No. 2 I have no copies.
The party is yet in the field,
having now arrived at
Lake Michigan, I expect.
Where am I going?
Don't ask me. To-day noon
I shall be in Ithaca; then
where, I know not.

Yours as ever,
L. H. Bailey

Michigan Agricultural College,

DEPARTMENT OF HORTICULTURE AND LANDSCAPE GARDENING.

Agricultural College P. O.,

Ingham Co., Mich. July 4 1888

My Dear Deane:

I send you to-day a small parcel of plants in a bundle sent to Mr. Watson. Call there for them before you go away. Avena Smithii was found on our northern trip, but the specimens are in Dr. Beal's hands. I will send you one later.

Exceedingly hot to-day. I have worked most of the day on my northern collections.

I have not heard from you recently but suppose that you are busy getting ready to be off.

Yours &c

L. H. Bailey

Michigan Agricultural College,

COLLEGE FACULTY:

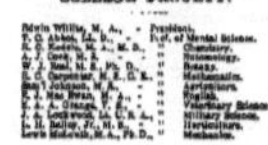
Edwin Willits, M. A., - President.
T. C. Abbot, LL. D., - Prof. of Mental Science.
R. C. Kedzie, M. A., M. D., " Chemistry.
A. J. Cook, M. S., " Entomology.
W. J. Beal, M. S., Ph. D., " Botany.
R. C. Carpenter, M. S., C. E., " Mathematics.
Sam'l Johnson, M. S., " Agriculture.
E. J. MacEwan, M. A., " English.
E. A. A. Grange, V. S., " Veterinary Science.
J. A. Lockwood, Lt. U. S. A., " Military Science.
L. H. Bailey, Jr., M. S., " Horticulture.
Lewis McLouth, M. A., Ph. D., " Mechanics.

DEPARTMENT OF HORTICULTURE AND LANDSCAPE GARDENING.

Agricultural College P. O.,
Ingham Co., Mich. July 18, 1888.

My Dear Deane:

My European plans are not very complete so far as routes are concerned and cannot be because I can not gather much information concerning the experiment stations, gardens, and some other things I desire to see. I hope to see all the important experiment stations of Europe — and there are many — all the leading botanic gardens, all the best parks and great horticultural places, and incidentally I shall look for the originals of

Michigan Agricultural College,

DEPARTMENT OF HORTICULTURE AND LANDSCAPE GARDENING.

Agricultural College P. O.,

Ingham Co., Mich., ...188....

can go and come at all times, seasonable and unseasonable. Moreover, I can leave any country or portion of my plan at one side if I find myself crowded for time, and can visit only the most conspicuous points of interest. I am not going to see sights, and shall not often turn aside for mere pleasure. I am going for business this time.

I have purchased my ticket for the Steamship Sardinian, sailing from Quebec Aug. 30 for Ireland. So far as I can determine now, my route will lie somewhat as follows: Ireland, Scotland, England, Wales, France, Belguim, Holland, Den-

Michigan Agricultural College,

DEPARTMENT OF HORTICULTURE AND LANDSCAPE GARDENING.

Agricultural College P. O.

3 Ingham Co. Mich. .... 188..

mark, Sweden, Germany, Switzer-land, Austria, Italy, and, Perhaps, Greece.

My sets of Carex are all broken up, so that I think I have less than a third of one left. Of some of the species I still have a number of specimens of the original finding. Of most I have duplicates of other collecting, however. Did you get your package?

Yours truly,
L. H. Bailey

I am taking many photographs, with unusual success, – practice for my trans-Atlantic tour.

—1888.—

EXERCISES OF

COMMENCEMENT WEEK.

Michigan State Agricultural College.

SUNDAY, AUGUST 12.

2:30 P. M.—Baccalaureate Address—Pres't Willits.

MONDAY, AUGUST 13.

8 P. M.—Literary Society Reunions and Banquets.

TUESDAY, AUGUST 14.

10 A. M.—COMMENCEMENT EXERCISES.

1 P. M.—Commencement Dinner.

3 to 5 P. M.—President's Reception.

8 P. M.—Senior Class-Day Exercises and Banquet.

WEDNESDAY, AUG. 15—ALUMNI DAY.

8 A. M.—Business Meeting.

~~9 A. M.—Class Meetings.~~

10:30 A. M.—Literary Exercises.

1 P. M.—Dinner.

~~3 P. M.—Adjourned Business Meeting.~~

7 P. M.—Banquet.

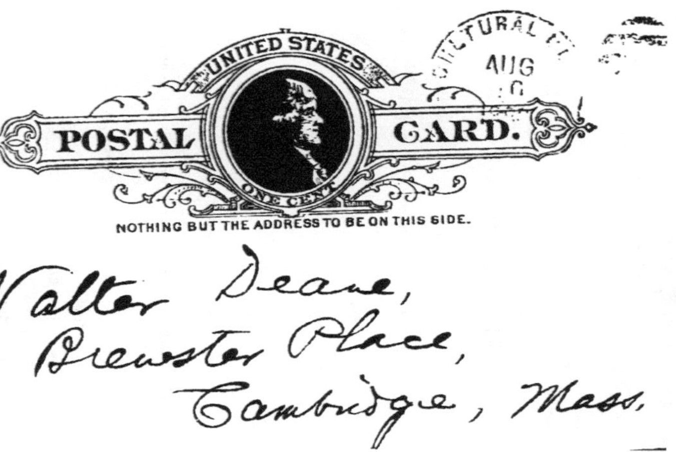

NOTHING BUT THE ADDRESS TO BE ON THIS SIDE.

Walter Deane,
Brewster Place,
Cambridge, Mass.

—1888.—

EXERCISES OF

COMMENCEMENT WEEK.

Michigan State Agricultural College.

SUNDAY, AUGUST 12.

2:30 P. M.—Baccalaureate Address—Pres't Willits.

MONDAY, AUGUST 13.

8 P. M.—Literary Society Reunions and Banquets.

TUESDAY, AUGUST 14.

10 A. M.—COMMENCEMENT EXERCISES.

1 P. M.—Commencement Dinner.

3 to 5 P. M.—President's Reception.

8 P. M.—Senior Class-Day Exercises and Banquet.

WEDNESDAY, AUG. 15—ALUMNI DAY.

8 A. M.—Business Meeting.

~~9 A. M.—Class Meetings.~~

10:30 A. M.—Literary Exercises.

1 P. M.—Dinner.

~~3 P. M.—Adjourned Business Meeting.~~

~~8~~ 7 P. M.—Banquet.

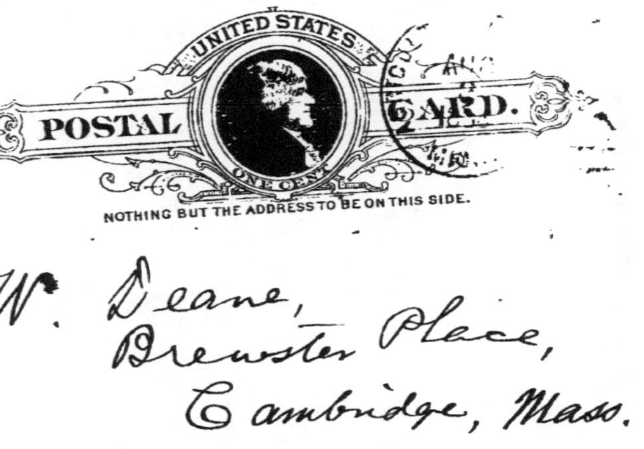
UNITED STATES
POSTAL CARD.
ONE CENT
NOTHING BUT THE ADDRESS TO BE ON THIS SIDE.
W. Deane,
Brewster Place,
Cambridge, Mass.

Michigan Agricultural College,

HORTICULTURAL DEPARTMENT.

Agricultural College P. O.
Ingham Co., Mich. Aug 14 1888

My Dear Deane:

I cannot understand why you should not find No. 2 of the articles in June 14 or 15 issues of the Free Press. No. 2 was written from W. Harrisville, June 13, and was entitled "A Dairyman's Paradise". I do not possess a copy of the article but it is preserved in the College record of the journey. I called at The Free Press office and bought the papers containing the articles, but they said ~~that~~ they had no copies left containing the second article. My last article was No. 7, a copy of which I send you.

I am to make a parting speech to the students & faculty this morning and I must hasten. Will let you know my address in time.

Yours
L. H. Bailey

CORNELL UNIVERSITY EXPERIMENT STATION,

ITHACA, N. Y.

L. R. ROBERTS, H. H. WING, E. L. WILLIAMS,

Horticultural Department.

L. H. BAILEY, PROFESSOR OF HORTICULTURE.

Lansing, Aug. 26, 1888

My Dear Deane:

Your welcome letter from Hyannisport is at hand. Tomorrow I leave my home and family for a long trip. Words can not describe the pang I feel at leaving them. I shall be very lonely in a strange land and I shall want to hear from all my friends. My English address is [illegible], 9 Strand, London. My continental address is 35 Boulevard des Capucines, Paris. Address my letters to London now, and I will inform you when to change. Let me hear from you often.

I do not know if any of the articles on the northern journey which followed mine can be had. I have never seen them and do not know in what issues they were published, although I know their [illegible].

Good bye, L. H. Bailey

Aug. 30, 1888.
7.30 P.M.

My Dear Deane:

This is my last chance to throw you a line before reaching The Emerald Isle. The pilot leaves us to-night and mail is taken off. I came aboard Tuesday night at Montreal. We are having a nice sail down a mighty and picturesque river.

I hope to reach Londonderry a week from to-morrow. Shall stop over there until I get straightened up — should I need straightening — and then go down to Dublin.

Good bye!

Yours in

L. H. Bailey

Dublin, Ireland,
~~Dec.~~ Sept 9, 1888.

My Dear Deane:

After 9½ days on ship, and a very rough passage across the sea, I found myself in Loch Foyle on the north coast of Ireland. A tender took off the few Ireland passengers and conveyed us to Londonderry, 20 miles down the Loch and river. Then did I open my eyes in a new world, even in the midst of an old one. Then did I begin to stare and so do I continue to do unto the present time. Things are so odd that I can scarcely realize their existence. I have seen Pat, — hundreds of him, — and an interesting person he is. Everything is done upon such a small scale in these parts, as an American measures, that I find it hard work to convince myself that people are in earnest. They seem to be playing. To enumerate all the strange things I see would be to enumerate everything I see. I am in hoary Dublin for the purpose of seeing Phoenix park, — said to be one of the best in the world, — and the Royal Botanic Gardens. To-day I took tram-cars, — riding on top! — and made preliminary visits to these places. But I am so immensely disappointed in the park that I shall not go there again. But the Botanic Gardens far exceed my expectations. They are immense, and very, very fine. I shall spend all day to-morrow there, making notes and taking pictures.

If to-morrow is fair and I progress as I hope to do, Tuesday I shall cross the Irish sea to Wales. Shall spend only a day or two there, and then go to Chatsworth, England, the seat of the Duke of Devonshire, said to be the finest estate in England. I shall then spend a few days in the vicinity of Birmingham, and then proceed to Kew. My route from there is not yet determined upon. I shall rely largely upon the directions given me there, and may change all my plans of the future.

Let me hear from you often.

Yours truly,

L. H. Bailey

My Dear Deane:

Yours of the 5th reached me Monday morning. I am now busily engaged at Kew, with the carices. I am going through Dr Boott's herb. particularly just now. It is interesting to find the originals of so many of our little known and puzzling species. C. Raeana, for instance, which has perplexed me so long, is nothing more nor less than slender C. monile. Even such a familiar species as C. cephaloidea must be overhauled. A year ago, I discovered that two things had been passed as this species, altho' no one has recognized the fact so far as I know. Boott's own herb. proves this conclusively. It is a great puzzle. The guess which I made in my last notes in Bot. Gaz. that Boott's first C. aperta is the plant known provisionally as C. acuta var. prolixa is correct; and I also find that the European var. prolixa is quite a different thing, as I had long suspected. So I shall raise the plant to specific rank as C. aperta.

But to tell you of all these things would be to describe almost every thing I see in the herbaria.

Dr Britton and wife are here, but go

home in a very few days. I shall dine with them to-night. Trelease is expected to call here this week on his way from Berlin.

My trip so far has been a delightful one. Every day has been as fine as one can expect of English weather. While in Wales I visited Hawarden Castle, and saw Mr. & Mrs. Gladstone & John Morley.

I hope to get through here next week, and shall then go to Scotland.

Drop me a line often.

Yours &c
L. H. Bailey

cluding some half dozen or more new species. Among the interesting herbaria I have consulted are those of Boott, Carey, Drummond, Goodenough, Rudge, Gay, Walter, Linnaeus, and Robt. Brown. By request, I am to publish a few notes before I return in the Journal of Botany.

I am glad to hear of Mrs. Deane's improvement. She must have had a serious time. Please convey my regards and congratulations to her.

I am getting anxious to get home and I may pick up my duds and skip at any time.

Write often. Yours &c. W.B.

Harpenden, England,
Oct. 6, 1888

My Dear Deane:

Your welcome letter of the 22nd. ult. reached me yesterday. You need not fear of boring me, for I am only too glad of letters from America.

So far I have had a delightful time, and have learned a great deal. I go to Oxford to-day, and will spend a couple days there. Then I go north to Chatsworth, the seat of the Duke of Devonshire, then to Edinburgh, and thence, the last of next week, across the North Sea to Norway.

I am in Harpenden to visit the famous agricultural experiment station of Rothamsted. The country about here is very attractive.

morning I hired a lad to carry my camera, and I went for a walk through the groves and by-ways. England is now as green and verdant as Massachusetts is in June. The air this morning is crisp and fragrant, and I enjoyed the walk immensely.

In London I made the following acquaintances: Sir J.D. Hooker, Prof. Oliver, B. Daydon Jackson, N. E. Brown, C. B. Clark, W. T. Thistleton Dyer, Geo. Nicholson, Wm. Carruthers, James Britten. I found them all pleasant and approachable men, particularly Mr. Clark, Mr. Carruthers and Mr. Britten. Mr. Clarke is monographing Cyperaceae for De Candolle. He has been at work a year and a half on Scirpus, and is not yet done with it.

I was twice at the Linnaean herbarium in Piccadilly. You can imagine how eagerly I looked over Linnaeus' plants, and other collections as well, for his insects, fishes, crustaceans, etc., are all there. I was particularly interested in his interleaved and annotated copies of his Species Plantarum. I took pictures of some of his plants. I will send you some finished pictures when I get home.

I have lots of Carex notes for publication, as soon as I return, in-distance to the marvellous blue of the Skager Rack. I have never enjoyed scenery so much as yesterday!

And now, this spicy and gleaming Sunday morning, I wait for a ship for Christiania. There I shall be as far north as southern Greenland. A day or two there, and then I cross Norway and Sweden to Upsala — the home of Linnaeus — and Stockholm, and then south to Copenhagen.

I hope that you are well and happy, and I trust that Mrs. D. is entirely recovered. Remember me to her.

I send you a few sprigs from the cliffs of Otterø, an island near here.

Yours truly ——
L. H. Bailey.

Kristianssand, Norway,
14 Oct. 1888.

My Dear Deane:

Now, indeed, do I find myself a stranger in a strange land. The Scotch ship upon which I had spent two days, nearly, upon the North Sea, steamed away down the Skager Rack towards Jutland, and left me alone and friendless, a stranger to the people and the language. I found a hotel, and a maid was presently [illegible]. I addressed her in English and she shook her head. Then I tried German, and again she shook her head. I sat down to await developments, Micawber-like.

Presently the maid said "Rum?" This I construed to mean room, and I nodded. Thereupon she conducted me to a pleasant but peculiar room. In compliment to her, and to my stomach — I gave her my one word of Norsk, Frokost (breakfast), and she in turn nodded. Having now come to a mutual understanding, we were both happy.

Oh, these are luscious autumn days away up here in the "Nordland"! The air appears to have been refined, purified of everything earthy, and I seemed all day yesterday to have lived in some ethereal state. I roamed in the most dreamy sort of way in winding paths by mountain springs and grassy dells, over beetling crags and by blue ponds [illegible] the embrace of rock. Everywhere the luscious air and the gleaming sunlight, and the mellow silence, charmed my soul, and seemed to eliminate from my spirit every passion and ambition! The dells are still green, and the heather is yet purple in the little vales and on the hillsides; and even yet a scarce [illegible] [illegible] hide their bloom under the rocks. From the crests I looked over a network of fjords and lakes, and away in the

Stockholm, Sweden, 18 Oct.
My Dear Deane: I have just returned
from Upsala, where I went to examine
Wahlenberg's carices. I found only a
part of them there. The remainder are said
to be here in Stockholm. I shall look them
up to-morrow. From here I go south to
Lund and Copenhagen. I saw Thunberg's
herb. at Upsala. Upsala is a fine old
university town. Your card of the 2nd is
just at hand. Glorious weather here.
I am well and happy. But I get lonely
and long to see an English woman.
Yours as ever, L. H. Bailey

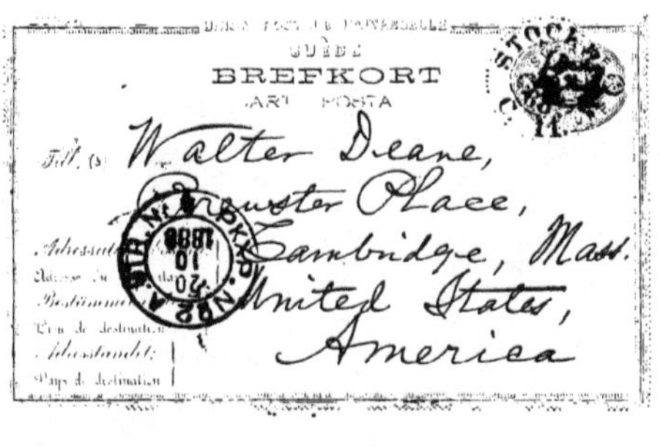

BREFKORT

Till Walter Deane,
Brewster Place,
Cambridge, Mass.
United States,
America

they are C. flexilis Rudge! No wonder Wahlenberg described the leaves as hairy!! There is a bare possibility that the remainder of Wahlenberg's things are here in Copenhagen. I shall find out.

I go to Berlin in two or three days, and there I shall find the originals of Muhlenberg, Willdenow, Kunth, Scheele and Boeckeler. Thence to Halle to see Schkuhr's, and then to Italy to find Allioni's. Returning to Paris, I shall see Michaux's, Lamarck's, and Steudel's. Then I do not know what more I can do for American Carex in Europe, for in Copenhagen I expect to see the plants of Drejer, Liebmann, and Lange. By the way,

Copenhagen, Denmark,
20 Oct. 1888.

My Dear Deane:

Arriving here to-night, I found your welcome letter of Sept. 30 and card of Oct. 7 waiting for me. It is a great pleasure to be able to hear from friends when one is so far from home, alone and among strange people and strange tongues.

In Sweden I have been chasing after Wahlenberg's Carices. I was surprised and disappointed not to find them at Upsala. Even Prof. Fries thought that all of Wahlenberg's things were in their collection. But such is not the case. His American species are not there. Most of his American species were made upon specimens which he saw in Swartz's herbarium, so I went to the Riksmuseum in

Stockholm to search among Swartz's plants. Some of his species I found, but C. grisea, C. prasina, C. latifolia, C. tribuloides, and some others, do not appear to be in existence. I am almost relieved to know that they are not, for fear that they might turn out as C. livida has, which I unfortunately found. I used the name C. livida because Wahlenberg himself, in Flora Lapponica, says that it is the same as C. livida. But it is not! It is C. tentaculata! So C. tentaculata becomes C. livida, and livida holds its own! I am sorry that such a change becomes necessary, but it cannot be avoided. I am finding many other snarls equal to this. But in all the changing, there is the satisfaction that we are constantly getting nearer the truth, and in most cases we are getting down to bed-rock. There is no going behind the names of Wahlenberg, so far as I know, for American species, except in the single instance of the work of Gunnerus.

But I am happy to have settled the C. castanea, about which so many elegant guesses have been made and so much good paper and ink wasted (see my Synopsis, p. 118, in proof thereof!). In the Riks-museum I unearthed the very originals, which have not been seen by a student of the genus from Wahlenberg's time until now, and work. I will unfold my ambitions to you when we meet.

I am much interested in your letters. The note concerning the Calluna was particularly interesting. Write as often as you can.

Dublin, London, Edinburgh, Kristiania, Stockholm, Copenhagen — six capitals; and which do I like best? For dullness, Dublin; for fog and dirt, London; for beauty and picturesqueness, Edinburgh (most beautiful and charming city!); for cleanliness, and briskness of atmosphere, Kristiania; for stability and method of laying out, for the physique and bearing of its men, Stockholm; for commercial snap, Copenhagen! Strange things I see as I fly!

Yours sincerely,
L. H. Bailey

however, I am going to Prague to see Presl's, some of which are unknown. The only remaining collection of particular interest to Americans is that of Meyer's at St. Petersburgh, but his figures are so good that there is not much necessity of seeing the plants. I had planned, however, to go to Russia, but time goes so rapidly that I gave it up.

But my flight in Europe is not to see Carex solely, altho', to tell the truth, I had little other business in Scandinavia. But my observation of the horticulture and agriculture of the country is of inestimable use to me, and I am feeling that I can make things tell when I get to work for myself again. I am full of my horticultural

Macoun tells us nothing new when he declares that the boreal Carices are not yet permanently named. I have not the least hope, even in my most sanguine moments, that they ever will be established. And I am confirmed in this opinion since I have been to Copenhagen and have studied the Greenland and Iceland specimens there. The Danes know more about these plants than anyone else, and the arctic herbarium at Copenhagen is very fine. Yet it is impossible to settle one's mind upon many of the species.

I have run hastily thro' Willdenow's herbarium, just to see what it contains. Next week I shall give it a thorough study. I noticed, however, that C. foenea has been entirely miscomprehended! I am sorry that the lightning strikes here, for straminea is bad enough now. C. refracta and C. juncea are going to give me trouble also. I am almost dreading to see the collections of Schkuhr, Michaux, and Lamarck for fear other species will be upset. Willdenow's herb. contains the types of Muhlenberg.

The people everywhere, in the herbaria, are very kind and give one every facility. Here at Berlin Dr. Schumann even divided Boeckeler's types of C. pilosiuscula with me, although they were mounted! And I have secured types of Alaskana, Krausei, and Urbani, as well.

Berlin, Oct. 26, 1888.

My dear Dean:

Yours of the 26th, crossed, stamped, and interlined almost beyond recognition, chased me down to-day. It finds me enjoying good health and strange sights, and queer things among the herbaria. I have been in Boeckeler's things all day, and the following are some of the points I have determined:

C. Alaskana = C. gynocrates

C. Krausei = C. capillaris

C. Saskatchewana = C. capillaris

C. Urbani = C. flava var.

C. Beyrichiana = C. tentaculata!

I find that even here at Berlin Boeckeler's work is not much thought of. His C. truncata, as I have no doubt told you before, is a form of C. laxiflora.

If I run across any local floras I will think of you. I must tell you of a streak of luck. I have long wanted to get Drejer's Caricum Criticum Borealium, but have never succeeded in getting track of a copy. Walking out in Copenhagen the other evening I went in front of a book store, and it occurred to me to go in and enquire for this book just for fun. I addressed the shop-keeper in German, and what did he do but bring me the book forthwith! I could scarcely believe my eyes! And he charged me only 80 öre (about 20 cts.) for it!

I shall be here a week or so, in the parks and gardens. Then I go south to Halle, Leipzig, etc. I hope that a month from now will find me about ready to take ship.

Yours truly,

L. H. Bailey

Berlin, 1 Nov., 1888

My Dear Deane: I drop you a line to tell you that you need not address any more letters to me in Europe. Next week I go down to Halle, Leipzig, Tharandt, Dresden and Prague, and thence south into Italy. I am not decided yet as to whether I shall go to Vienna. I do not know as there is any thing of particular interest to me there, and I cannot gad about for the fun of it.

No one will know our carices by the time I have published the results of my study here.

C. foenea Willd. = C. argyrantha Tuckm!

C. varia Muhl. = C. Emmonsii Dew!

C. refracta = C. tenax Reuter! This refracta-castanea muddle has been the worst puzzle we have had. I settled the castanea part of it in Stockholm. Both Willd. and Schk. record C. refracta from Mt. Cenis, but Sprengel and all later botanists have said that the authors were mistaken, that the plant must be American because no such plant grows in Europe. Moreover, Willdenow's specimens are ticketed "Pennsylvania, Muhl." But I have identified it with a plant discovered some over twenty years ago in the Alps of Piedmont, and described in a local Italian journal as tenax by Reuter. How strange that during all those years, the plant should have been unknown! Reuter's plant does not exist in the herbaria here, and it was by the merest chance that Prof. Ascherson had a specimen of it in his own hands, — just rec'd!

C. juncea, founded upon a garden plant, and said to have come from America, is not American at all, but = C. ferruginea Scop.!

C. OEderi has been misunderstood, also.

I shall be anxious to hear the result of our presidential election, but I suppose that I shall know nothing of it until two or three weeks after it has taken place. My news will come through letters from home, for the papers in these parts seem to know nothing of America. I seem like a half-forgotten being, wandering because I have no other occupation. The Americans have now gone home, and I have no companionship whatever.

The weather is still warm here, and the leaves are not all off the trees.

(Remember me to Mrs. Deane.

Yours truly, as ever,

L. H. Bailey

Willd. is C. Pennsylvanica, but in Hb. Folk. is what we have called C. varia! But Folk. figured Willdenow's plant, so that Willd's plant must be taken as the type. C. varia in Hb. Folk., as in Hb. Willd., is good C. Emmonsii. It is not strange that Dr Torrey and Dr Gray did not rightly understand C. varia and Emmonsii, for both these groups were imperfectly known then. It was not until 1840 that C. adusta was separated, and then for many years it was misunderstood.

I have rec'd every one of your letters, I think.

Remember me to Mrs. D. I shall not invite you to write me, and I am glad that I shall not! L. H. B.

Leipzig, Nov. 7 1888

My dear Deane:

Yours of the 21st of Oct. is mine. I was glad to hear of you. How precious are news from America and my friends in this far off land! Or rather, I had better say, in these lands! I saw America upon a large map today and the picture assured me that it does exist, and is not the land of dreams which it all but seems to me! One by one the cities and the countries which I have known only as points and patches of color on my atlas, become real to me. Saxony is no longer a patch upon my map, but an extent of real soil, populated by the most provincial of Dutchmen. Day after to-morrow I shall reach Hungary if all goes well. Then I pull out for Italy, making the passage of the Alps through the Tyrol by way of Innsbruck. I am about deciding to shorten up my trip, for I have nearly seen enough of the country and its horticulture for my present purpose. I must still see the plants of Allioni (at Turin) and those of Steudel, Michaux and Lamarck, and I shall take in the garden- ing of the places I visit in so doing; then I shall go home.

At Halle, among Schkuhr's carices, I found a note left by Dr. Gray, Aug. 2, 1839! Some of Schkuhr's species do not exist, unless they are at Philadelphia among Muhlenberg's things. C. tetanica is one, and Sch. variata another. I particularly wanted to see them. Schk. and Willd. saw each others proofs, and they wrote back and forth, and it is difficult to decide which has priority. The C. mar- ginata of Muhl. [illegible]

Boston, dec 11 188

I left Mr. Watson's umbrella at your house. Will you please take it to the garden when you go over?

I leave at 3 on B&A.

Yours

L. H. B.

UNITED STATES

POSTAL CARD.

NOTHING BUT THE ADDRESS TO BE ON THIS SIDE.

Walter Deane,
Brewster Place,
Cambridge

Vienna, Austria, Nov. 10. 188

My Dear Deane: I am thus far on my way towards Venice. Distances are great in these parts. The country is very strange to me. At Prag I saw Presl's plants, and another one of my elegant guesses has collapsed, for C. anthericoides is C. macrocephala Willd! My objective point in Italy is Turin, to see Allioni's plants. A telegram in a native paper at Prag, from N.Y., says that Harrison is elected. I am surprised.

Yours &c L.H. Baile

WELTPOST-VEREIN (UNION POSTALE UNIVERSELLE).

CORRESPONDENZ-KARTE (CARTE POSTALE)

(ADMINISTRATION D'AUTRICHE.)

An Walter Deane,
Brewster Place,
Cambridge, Mass.
United States, Amerika.

Ithaca Dec. 28. 1888

My Dear Deane:

We arrived here last night, in good condition. For the present we inhabit a hotel, but hope to get settled during the week. Merry Christmas from both of us to yourself & Mrs. D.

Yours truly, L. H. Bailey.

UNITED STATES
POSTAL CARD
NOTHING BUT THE ADDRESS TO BE ON THIS SIDE
N. Y.
Walter Deane,
Brewster Place,

Lansing, [illegible] 188[illegible]

My dear Dr. [illegible] just home last night [illegible] [illegible] [illegible] [illegible] [illegible] [illegible] [illegible] [illegible] [illegible]

Please tell me what the [illegible] phrase [illegible] $S.S.$ is, meaning [illegible] [illegible] the [illegible] [illegible] [illegible] a legitimate term for "ye [illegible] stigma", adj.? Address to Ithaca, [illegible]

Yours L. H. Bailey

Walter Deane,
Brewster Place,
Cambridge, Mass.

Ithaca, N.Y., Dec. 24, 1888

My Dear Deane:

At the University I found your letter of the 18th. I am obliged to you for the information. I had forgotten, if I ever knew, that Dr Gray had explained the v.s.

Yes, C. tribuloides v. moniliformis is the same as var. reducta. I at first intended to use the name moniliformis, as Tuckm. and Olney had done (under C. scoparia and C. lagopodioides), but when I found that var. moniliformis of C. straminea must stand, I changed the name under C. tribuloides to avoid confusion. I think that C. straminea var. moniliformis is a good species.

C. distans Linn. Sp. Pl. —? I do not know the page, and have not the means for finding out just now, as my books are not yet unpacked. But you can easily find the reference at the gardens. C. retrocurva var. copulata was never published and never will be. It was distributed by me as such in my sets, but I now know that it is a form of C. digitalis and I shall therefore describe it as var. copulata of that species.

I find much work ahead of me. In addition to 3 lectures to students each week, I am to give some ten or a dozen lectures throughout the State during the next two or three mos.

Let me hear of you often.

Yours truly, L. H. Bailey

Cornell University,
ITHACA, N. Y.

Dec. 26, 1888.

My Dear Friend:
Your remembrance reached me yesterday, and was very welcome. I sent you this morning a picture of baby.

When you go again to the gardens will you copy for me Nuttall's description of Carex filifolia, Genera N. Amer. Plants, ii. 204, and give me the habitat as recorded by Nuttall. I have never been able to find the original of this species. Nuttall's plants are at the British Museum, but this species is not among them. I have just got Schweinitz's plants, and among them is C. filifolia from Nuttall, but it is not at all the species we have taken it to be. I do not yet know if this is a type specimen.

We are now pleasantly settled at 23 Quarry St., where you may address my mail.

Happy new year to you and yours, from us both.

Yours truly,

L. H. Bailey

Horticultural Department of Cornell University Experiment Station.

L. H. BAILEY.

Ithaca, N. Y., Dec. 30 1888.

Dear Deane;

Yes, I will remit the $5.00 for the books in a few days, and shall be glad to get them. Thanks for your trouble. Send me your Carex conjuncta, and I will examine it and return. It is very rare. Baby's picture was taken about 10 days before Christmas. It is not very good. Hope you had a pleasant visit with W. W. Bailey. Shall begin to write on my new Carex paper to-morrow or Tuesday. Yours

L. H. Bailey

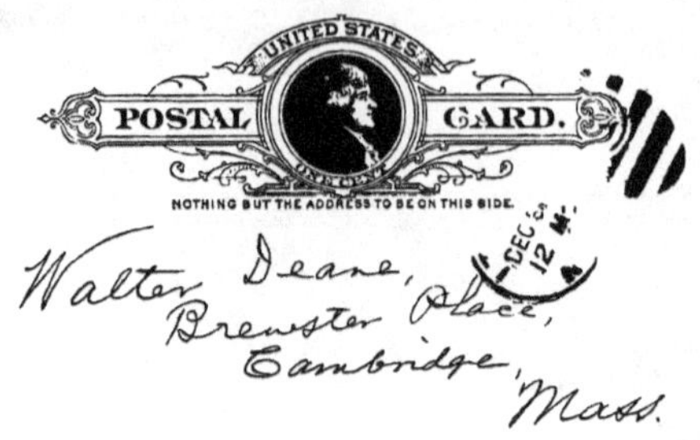
UNITED STATES
POSTAL CARD.
ONE CENT
NOTHING BUT THE ADDRESS TO BE ON THIS SIDE.
DEC
12
Walter Deane,
Brewster Place,
Cambridge,
Mass.

ITHACA, N. Y., Dec., 31st., 1888.

My Dear DEANE:- Your note concerning Carex filifolia is at hand, and is very welcome.The description shows that the plant that is so labelled in Herb. Schweinitz isnot the plant intended by Nuttall. The plant of Schweinitz is our poor old unfortunate much-to-be-pitied and everlastingly-knocked-about Carex varia of all authors except the one who made the species'

Poor Carex varia! Its feet are knocked from under it, and it stands in mid-air, without even the poor consolation of a name. And yet it may have a name; for Liebmann did so provoking a thing as to describe a weakling from uncivilized Mexico asCarex turbinata,_ a plant for all the world like an aberrant form of our unhappy species. It seems hard to be obliged to go to Mexico for a Christian na me, and yet I suppose that stranger things have happened. But time and more study must decide if we must adopt the name of the Dane.

But this is only one of two dozen or more delectable problemhich await those who, Nebuchadneezer-like, go to grass. (The word just above this is not Bohemian, but is simply a figurative expression which means "problems which").
Have I anything on my hands? Only this,- and twice as much more! A greenhouse to build; ten or twelve off-hand lectures to inflict upon innocent people in various parts of the virtuous state of New York; a lecture at Albany, Jan. 18th., on "A SEED: A chapter of suggestions",- a very suggestive subject and one which must be wellenough presented to appear in merciless print; three lectures a week to sleeping students;and a most undigestible lot of Carex pastry.

I have owed you a grudge for several months, and nowI have paid you off.

Yours, as ever,

L. H. Bailey

requests the pleasure of your presence at the

Commencement Exercises

August 14th 15th 16th & 17th 1887

www.ingramcontent.com/pod-product-compliance
Lightning Source LLC
Chambersburg PA
CBHW051724300426
44115CB00007B/448

* 9 7 8 3 3 3 7 3 9 3 6 3 2 *